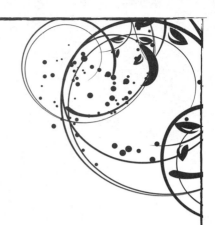

Get Wisdom!

MARILYN HICKEY

Get Wisdom!

Journal

MARILYN HICKEY MINISTRIES

Get Wisdom Journal

Marilyn Hickey Ministries
P.O. Box 6598
Englewood, Colorado 80155-6598

Printed in the United States of America
ISBN 978-0-9820515-0-4

Unless otherwise indicated, all Scripture quotations
are taken from the *New King James Version* of the Bible.

mhmin.org

Introduction

Every one of us stands at the brink of a major crisis at some point in our lives. During those times, we desperately need the wisdom of God. God's wisdom helps us to rise to a higher level of living and brings fulfillment of His ultimate purpose in our everyday lives.

Proverbs 4:7 exhorts us: *"Wisdom is the principal thing."* In other words, wisdom is the key. It's the key to solving your financial problems. It's the key to walking in the healing power of Jesus. It's the key to making your relationships work. Wisdom is the key to successful living. *"Therefore, get wisdom."*

The question is "How? How do we get this wisdom?" The Bible contains God's ultimate wisdom for your life. Psalms, Proverbs, Song of Solomon, Ecclesiastes, and Job, as well as the New Testament book of James, are considered to be the wisdom books. Each shows a different aspect of wisdom and that's what you are going to discover through the pages of this book.

Get Wisdom is not just a journal, a place to record your thoughts about wisdom; it's an interactive daily devotional. Each day begins with a scripture to meditate on, along with a question to journal about. The devotional focuses on everyday issues regarding finances, health, and relationships, and ends with a practical application exercise. At the conclusion of each day, there are several scriptures for you to speak over your life. This is such an important part—don't just read them. You need to speak the wisdom of God over every area of your life.

We all need more of God's wisdom in some area of our lives. So what are you waiting for? Start your journey today… *Get Wisdom!*

DAY 1

Get Wisdom

THREE KINDS OF WISDOM

WISDOM FOR TODAY

Wisdom is the principal thing; therefore get wisdom.
And in all your getting, get understanding.
Exalt her, and she will promote you;
She will bring you honor, when you embrace her.
She will place on your head an ornament of grace;
A crown of glory she will deliver to you.
Proverbs 4:7-9

Do you already have favorite books of the Bible to draw wisdom from?

Proverbs - James

What is your favorite scripture?

Pro. 3:16

GET WISDOM

Do you believe that Godly wisdom could bring
an answer to every problem in your life? Think about it.
Could God give you wisdom that would absolutely bring
a turnaround in your finances? Could Godly wisdom give
you an answer to your relationship problems? Could Godly
wisdom give you an answer to your physical and health
problems? Is there wisdom that can be applied in every
area of your life to make your life better?

I believe wisdom is the key for success in our
relationships, health, and finances.

The book of Proverbs confirms that wisdom is the
key that unlocks the door to success.

Wisdom is the principal thing; therefore get Wisdom.
Proverbs 4:7

You may be asking yourself, "How do I get wisdom?"
How did Solomon, perhaps the wisest man who ever lived,
acquire his wisdom? Did you know that all he did was ASK for
it? That's right! At the beginning of Solomon's reign, God told
Solomon he could ask for whatever he wanted. Solomon asked
for wisdom and knowledge to properly rule God's people.

*On that night God appeared to Solomon, and said to
him, "Ask! What shall I give you?" And Solomon said
to God: "You have shown great mercy to David my
father, and have made me king in his place. Now, O
LORD God, let Your promise to David my father be*

*established, for You have make me king over a people
like the dust of the earth in multitude. Now give me
wisdom and knowledge, that I may go out and come in
before this people; for who can judge this great people
of Yours?"* 2 Chronicles 1:7-10 NKJV

The Lord was delighted with Solomon, who
illustrated by his choice that he already had great wisdom.
A man who put God first and who was more concerned for
others than himself could be trusted with great blessing.
Therefore, God not only gave Solomon the wisdom he
requested, but riches, wealth, and honor such as no other
person ever possessed:

*Then God said to Solomon: "Because this was in
your heart, and you have not asked riches or wealth or
honor or the life of your enemies, nor have you asked
long life— but have asked wisdom and knowledge for
yourself, that you may judge My people over whom
I have made you king, wisdom and knowledge are
granted to you; and I will give you riches and wealth
and honor, such as none of the kings have had who
were before you, nor shall any after you have the like."*
2 Chronicles 1:11-13

That was Solomon and that was thousands of
years ago. So the question is, "How do you and I get
wisdom today?"

GET WISDOM

*If any of you lacks wisdom, let him ask of God,
who gives to all liberally and without reproach,
and it will be given to him. James 1:5.*

So the first step to acquiring wisdom is to ASK for it.

One day I was seated by a man on a plane who watched me intently as I was studying my Bible. When he asked me my occupation, I told him that I taught the Bible on television and in Buddhist, Hindu, and Muslim countries. He explained that he found it very difficult to believe that Jesus was the only way to salvation. I hear this all the time from people who often have a difficult time understanding the fundamental truth of the gospel.

I immediately asked God to give me the right words to say. The Lord simply told me to share my personal experience of how one prayer at the age of 16 changed my life—and that it's still changing my life six decades later. I told him about the power of Jesus' blood to forgive sins and how He became the Lord of my life through that one prayer.

THREE KINDS OF WISDOM

The man began to cry and explained that he had just been diagnosed with cancer and he wanted to know more about the prayer of salvation. I was so encouraged. It proved once again that when you ask for wisdom—God gives it— even flying at 33,000 feet.

This series on wisdom is where you and I live—and it's where we can live better. Open up your heart and mind and watch as God pours His wisdom into us!

What are 5 things you would do with your life if you were as wise as King Solomon?

1. _____

_____

_____

2. _____

_____

_____

3. _____

_____

_____

4. _____

_____

_____

5. _____

_____

_____

Reflections

Today I am speaking these words over my life:

I am wise. I hear the Lord's voice. I am increasing in learning and becoming a man/woman of understanding.*

I will be joyful in the Lord, He gives me wisdom and understanding.**

_____

_____

_____

_____

_____

_____

_____

_____

_____

_____

_____

_____

_____

_____

_____

_____

*Proverbs 1:5   **Proverbs 3:13.*

Reflections

DAY 2

3 Kinds of Wisdom

THREE KINDS OF WISDOM

WISDOM FOR TODAY

When wisdom enters your heart,
And knowledge is pleasant to your soul,
Discretion will preserve you;
Understanding will keep you. Proverbs 2:10-11

What is the single greatest obstacle that hinders your quest for wisdom?

_____

_____

_____

_____

List three things you can do TODAY to overcome that obstacle and three things you can do to make it a permanent part of your lifestyle.

1. _____

_____

_____

2. _____

_____

_____

3. _____

_____

_____

_____

3 Kinds of Wisdom

By definition, wisdom is the ability to judge soundly and deal prudently with facts. Wisdom is the successful use of knowledge. Intellectuals are known by what they *know*, but wise people are known by what they *do*. Wisdom will direct our thoughts, control our tongues, guide our steps, and protect our way:

> *I, wisdom, dwell with prudence, and find out knowledge and discretion. The fear of the LORD is to hate evil; Pride and arrogance and the evil way and the perverse mouth I hate. Counsel is mine, and sound wisdom; I am understanding, I have strength. By me kings reign, and rulers decree justice. By me princes rule, and nobles, all the judges of the earth.*
> Proverbs 8:12-16

There are three Greek words used in the New Testament which are all translated "wisdom": *Sophia*, *Phronesis*, and *Sunesis*. These three types of wisdom deal with the past, present, and future. *Sunesis* would include the past, *Phronesis* deals with the present, and *Sophia* takes us into the future. Together, they spell success in handling all of life.

When King Solomon prayed for wisdom, he asked for *Sophia* and *Phronesis* wisdom. First, he wanted *Sophia* or "big picture" wisdom. He needed to see ahead and know what was best for his nation. *Sophia* wisdom is the ability to discern what is happening in a situation and to look ahead, with hope, to a bright future. This kind of wisdom "sees through" a matter and inspires faith, hope, and patience.

Phronesis is "how to" wisdom. Solomon needed practical wisdom on how to deal with people and himself on a day-to-day basis. There's a story in First Kings that exemplifies the depth of Solomon's grasp of practical wisdom. Two mothers came to Solomon to settle a dispute about custody of a child. Each woman claimed they were the mother. Remember how Solomon discovered the mother's identity?

> *Then the king said, "Bring me a sword." So they brought a sword before the king. And the king said, "Divide the living child in two, and give half to one, and half to the other." Then the woman whose son was living spoke to the king, for she yearned with compassion for her son; and she said, "O my lord, give her the living child, and by no means kill him!" But the other said, "Let him be neither mine nor yours, but divide him." So the king answered and said, "Give the first woman the living child, and by no means kill him; she is his mother." 1 Kings 3:24-27*

At that moment, Solomon needed to know "how to" resolve the dispute. The Bible says get wisdom and then get understanding with it. Why do wisdom and understanding go together? Because we can get wisdom for a situation, but if we don't know how to apply the wisdom and we don't have the understanding of how to make it work—we're no better off than before.

Let me share something from my own family that helped me be a better parent. When Sarah was about 16 years old, a lot of her friends in high school drank alcohol. This was a great concern to me. One day I offered to help clean out her car and when I opened her car door, two beer cans rolled out. I immediately started to cry. I couldn't believe that my 16 year-old daughter, a Spirit-filled, born-again Christian was drinking alcohol.

Sarah began to explain how intense the peer pressure was at school. When I asked why she didn't talk to me about it, she said, "Because mom, you never listen to me. All you do is preach to me!" Well, she was right. If she ever came to me about a problem, I just preached, preached, preached, and never let her unwind or vent her frustrations. I knew at that moment I needed wisdom and the ability to understand my daughter's feelings like never before.

The Holy Spirit immediately showed me that I had to become more than a mother and pastor to Sarah. That day, I realized I had to become her friend as well as a better listener.

At the beginning, it was hard. She would come home late at night wanting to talk so I'd drag myself out of bed and listen to her talk. Sometimes I was shocked at what she said but I wouldn't say a word. After she finished she

THREE KINDS OF WISDOM

would ask me what I thought. That's how she began inviting me into her life, and as a result, she became open to receive the things I shared with her.

Today, Sarah is a mother of three and she still calls me to unwind and to seek my advice. Because I asked God for wisdom and understanding on how to become a better friend and listener to my daughter, we now have a wonderful mother-daughter relationship.

What situation in your life do you need wisdom for today?

_____

_____

_____

_____

_____

_____

_____

_____

_____

_____

_____

_____

_____

_____

_____

_____

_____

Reflections

Today I am speaking these words over my life:

I have a renewed mind and I meditate on
the Word daily.*

I will store the Word of God in my heart and He will make
that truth wisdom.**

_____
_____
_____
_____
_____
_____
_____
_____
_____
_____
_____
_____
_____
_____
_____
_____
_____

*Ephesians 4:23-24.   **Psalm 119:27

Reflections

DAY 3

Big Picture Wisdom

THREE KINDS OF WISDOM

WISDOM FOR TODAY

And we know that all things work together for good to those who love God, to those who are the called according to His purpose. Romans 8:28

How do you see God working in your life?

_____

_____

_____

_____

_____

_____

_____

_____

_____

Do you see a clear call from the Lord in your life?

_____

_____

_____

_____

_____

_____

_____

_____

_____

Big Picture Wisdom

When I began to study the wisdom of God, I memorized the book of Proverbs. I wanted both wisdom and understanding operating in my life. The Greek translation of the Old Testament word for wisdom is *Sophia*. I call it "big picture" wisdom.

Perhaps you've heard the old adage, "I can't see the forest for the trees." That's the heart of a man or woman crying out for *Sophia* wisdom. So many times our eyes and energy are focused on the calamity or crisis in front of us. The question we need to stop and ask ourselves is, "What's the big picture? Why am I facing this crisis and what does it have to do with God's plan for my life?" When God reveals the "big picture wisdom" for our lives He gives us the faith, perseverance, and patience necessary to fulfill God's plan— and not give up when adversity strikes.

During a trial it's necessary to have *Sophia* wisdom in order to understand what is happening and why. We also need to see beyond our trial in order to hope for a good outcome. Each of us needs to have *Sophia* wisdom to see all our situations to a successful outcome:

> *"For I know the plans I have for you," declares the LORD, "plans to prosper you and not to harm you, plans to give you hope and a future."* Jeremiah 29:11

THREE KINDS OF WISDOM

Ecclesiastes Chapter 3 teaches us what our life is going to be like and says something very important in its verses about *Sophia* wisdom. It says:

There is a time for everything, and a season for every activity under heaven:

a time to be born and a time to die, a time to plant and a time to uproot, a time to kill and a time to heal, a time to tear down and a time to build, a time to weep and a time to laugh, a time to mourn and a time to dance, a time to scatter stones and a time to gather them, a time to embrace and a time to refrain, a time to search and a time to give up, a time to keep and a time to throw away, a time to tear and a time to mend, a time to be silent and a time to speak, a time to love and a time to hate, a time for war and a time for peace.
Ecclesiastes 3:1-8 NIV

It's important for us to understand that God sees every season of our lives—and that He has a purpose for each season. He sees the big picture. But if you're like me, you want every season to be as smooth as silk, full of beauty and joy—no pain or suffering. Well, life isn't like that.

If you closely examine each verse of Ecclesiastes Chapter 3, you'll see every facet of life discussed. As you look at each contrast you'll discover there are going to be seasons of sowing—with no harvest in sight.

Big Picture Wisdom

This might be followed by a season of pruning and pulling
out weeds in your life like jealousy, pride, and lust. Then
you might be confronted with a season filled with patience.
All this comes before a season of harvest.

At the heart of Solomon's writings in Ecclesiastes
is the realization that timings, seasons, and the contrast
of seasons make up the big picture, the *Sophia* wisdom of
God. God is saying, "Look to me and know that I am the
ultimate wisdom through every season." When you have
God's *Sophia* wisdom operating in your life, you understand
that each season is a part of God's big picture for your
life—and He is working through every season—and all for
your good!

> *And we know that all things work together for good*
> *to those who love God, to those who are the called*
> *according to His purpose.* Romans 8:28

There's something else to remember that's very
important in the big picture. *Sophia* wisdom has, at its core,
goal setting. *Sophia* requires that you set goals in order to
have something for which to use your faith to stay victorious
during each season. But it is important that you have
God's wisdom in setting these goals. Otherwise, you might
start aiming at and believing for things that were never in
God's plans for your life—or even worse, you might start
taking shortcuts. Remember, there's a time and season for
everything under the sun.

THREE KINDS OF WISDOM

What are your goals for the next five years?

_____
_____
_____
_____
_____
_____
_____

What are your goals for the next ten years?

_____
_____
_____
_____
_____
_____
_____

What are your goals for the next twenty years?

_____
_____
_____
_____
_____
_____
_____

Reflections

Today I am speaking these words over my life:

I will keep my eyes on the goal and not let anything distract me from my right path.*

I will build my life on the Rock.**

*Proverbs 4:25   **Psalm 104:18

Reflections

DAY 4

God's "How to" Wisdom

THREE KINDS OF WISDOM

WISDOM FOR TODAY

And God is able to make all grace abound toward you, that you, always having all sufficiency in all things, may have an abundance for every good work.
2 Corinthians 9:8

Have you ever been in a situation where you've cried out, "God, I don't know what to do?" Describe how you felt and what you did next.

_____

_____

_____

_____

_____

_____

_____

_____

_____

_____

_____

_____

_____

_____

_____

_____

_____

_____

God's "How To" Wisdom

Let's take a look at the second kind of wisdom—
Phronesis wisdom. Why is it important? *Phronesis* is "how
to" wisdom and it's very practical. It is the kind of wisdom
that knows what to do in any circumstance.

We can have the big picture for our children, for
example. We want them to go through high school and to
graduate from college and succeed in life. That's the big
picture. But how do you get them through grade school,
high school, and college? You might want to be a gourmet
chef. But how are you going to prosper financially until
you get the training and experience? One of your goals
in life might be to stay strong and healthy. That's the big
picture. But how are you going to do it? How do you get
Phronesis wisdom?

> *Hear instruction and be wise, and do not disdain it.*
> *Blessed is the man who listens to me, watching daily*
> *at my gates, waiting at the posts of my doors. For*
> *whoever finds me finds life, and obtains favor from the*
> LORD. Proverbs 8:33-35

God wants to reveal His plan for your life. You need
to seek him for the "how to." Spend time with Him — He
will show you what to do in every situation.

THREE KINDS OF WISDOM

I get my manicures at a nail salon owned by three Vietnamese sisters. They have a statue of Buddha prominently displayed in their salon. When I sought the Lord for wisdom on how to share Jesus with the staff, He gave me a very simple solution. I found out they love chocolate—so I started bringing them gifts of chocolate every time I had my nails done. That really got their attention and helped build relationships. One day I invited them to a home Bible study group for a lasagna dinner. They had never been to church but they came to my Bible study. Well, two of them are now born again. I lovingly call them my Vietnamese daughters. God knows how to reach people and He'll give us keys of wisdom that will unlock their hearts if we ask Him. With these women it all started with gifts of chocolate.

When Solomon prayed in 2 Chronicles 1:10, he prayed for wisdom, but he also acknowledged that he needed God's knowledge for just the basic, simple things. God gave it to him. The Bible is very practical. All throughout Proverbs and James, for example, there are nuggets of knowledge for everyday living! If you need answers to situations in your life, there's no better place to start.

GOD'S "HOW TO" WISDOM

What area of your life do you need how-to *Phronesis* wisdom
the most? How will you get it?

_____

_____

_____

_____

_____

_____

_____

_____

_____

_____

_____

_____

_____

_____

_____

_____

_____

_____

_____

_____

_____

_____

_____

_____

_____

_____

_____

Reflections

Today I am speaking these words over my life:

I will be directed by the light of God's Word.*

I will study God's Word for the right and good
kind of knowledge.**

_____

_____

_____

_____

_____

_____

_____

_____

_____

_____

_____

_____

_____

_____

_____

_____

_____

_____

* Proverbs 4:26   ** 1 Samuel 2:3

DAY 5

Networking Wisdom

THREE KINDS OF WISDOM

WISDOM FOR TODAY

Two are better than one, because they have a good reward for their labor. For if they fall, one will lift up his companion. But woe to him who is alone when he falls, for he has no one to help him up. Ecclesiastes 4:9-10

What does the word "networking" mean to you? How have you applied it in your life?

_____

_____

_____

_____

_____

_____

_____

How do you know when that new person in your life was sent by God?

_____

_____

_____

_____

_____

_____

_____

Networking Wisdom

The third word for wisdom is *Sunesis*. This is networking wisdom. First, God gives you the big picture. Then He gives you the how to, but you need the people and the circumstances to flow together to make it work. So God networks people into your life to help fulfill your destiny.

Did you know that God knows how to network the right people into your life at the right time? He knows exactly the right person, the right circumstance, the right book, or the right sermon to help you grow. God knows how to bring the right friends into your life to sharpen you. There is a process with *Sunesis* and there are no shortcuts. It is critical that we understand what God can do through others. Only God can bring the person to help accomplish what He wants you to do in your life. We'll fail if we try to manipulate people to achieve our goals.

Throughout my years of ministry God has brought men and women into my life who made it possible for me to fulfill the "big picture" for my life. I learned to always be sensitive to these "divine appointments." We've all had them. It's that special time when God directs someone to cross our paths that will make an indelible mark on our future. I've learned to never turn away from people God brought into my life. It's God's *Sunesis* wisdom in operation.

THREE KINDS OF WISDOM

Many years ago I started teaching at home Bible studies. A man who trained corporate leaders to speak in public came to my Bible study. At that time I had just started teaching on the radio and this man offered to help me improve my speaking skills. It turned out he was part of *Sunesis* wisdom in my life. Although he was very demanding, he taught me so much. To this day I thank God for networking that man into my life.

God's networking wisdom inspires growth and maturity. Wisdom is the foundation of every achievement, the instrument of peace in every relationship (including our relationship with God), the source of wisdom for our finances, our health, and guidance for our daily lives. The measure of wisdom we use affects our attitudes and behavior, determines our choices, and steers the course of our lives. When we open up our hearts and minds, God will give us *Sophia*, *Phronesis*, and *Sunesis* wisdom everywhere and for every situation.

NETWORKING WISDOM

Who has made the most dramatic impact on your life? Why?

_____

_____

_____

_____

_____

_____

_____

_____

_____

_____

_____

_____

_____

_____

_____

_____

_____

_____

_____

_____

_____

_____

_____

_____

_____

_____

_____

_____

_____

_____

_____

_____

Reflections

Today I am speaking these words over my life:

I will seek first His righteousness and He will take care of everything else.*

I plant God's Word in the lives of others and I gain a great return. **

DAY 6

The Pursuit

THREE KINDS OF WISDOM

WISDOM FOR TODAY

But the wisdom that is from above is first pure, then peaceable, gentle, willing to yield, full of mercy and good fruits, without partiality and without hypocrisy.
James 3:16-17

The book of James is known as the New Testament "Proverbs." In what ways is it different and in what ways is it similar to Proverbs?

_____

_____

_____

_____

_____

_____

How much time each day do you pursue God's wisdom for your life? List 5 things you could do to increase your pursuit of wisdom.

_____

_____

_____

_____

_____

_____

THE PURSUIT

In recent years the bookshelves of department, grocery, and convenience stores have been filled with "how to" books for the "do-it-yourself" generation. Today, a person can learn from a book or the Internet how to do everything from refinishing antique furniture to building a yacht.

Long ago, God cornered the market on "how to" books when He gave us His Word. The Bible is the book of answers. It shows us the "big picture" wisdom. The book of Proverbs and the New Testament book of James are packed with some of the greatest treasures of "how to" wisdom. The Old Testament is full of examples of "networking" wisdom. If you are pursuing wisdom for a particular situation, search through the books of the Bible.

> *My son, if you accept my words and store up my commands within you, turning your ear to wisdom and applying your heart to understanding, and if you call out for insight and cry aloud for understanding, and if you look for it as for silver and search for it as for hidden treasure, then you will understand the fear of the LORD and find the knowledge of God. For the LORD gives wisdom, and from his mouth come knowledge and understanding.*
> Proverbs 2:1-6 NIV

Three kinds of Wisdom

God will give you wisdom from his Word. Then you have to apply it to your life. Sometimes that means just saying what He says. A woman who works at the ministry shared her testimony with me about her firstborn son. When she became pregnant, she decided to have a home birth. She read every book on childbirth she could find. But she didn't stop there. She searched the scriptures for every word on childbirth; then she wrote them out in first person and spoke those words over her and her baby every day.

When she went into labor, the midwife came and stayed with her through 24 hours of labor. When her son was finally born, he was not breathing. There was no life in him. She could have cried out, "Oh, my God, my baby is dead" and blamed God for the death of her baby; but instead she cried out to God and reminded Him of what His Word says, that *"every good and perfect gift is from above"* (James 1:7), that *"God does not take away life"* (2 Sam 14:14) but He is the giver of life. God had given her the wisdom to speak the truth over that situation and because she did, God breathed the Spirit of life back into that baby, and she witnessed a miracle. This year her son will be 30 years old.

Get wisdom! Get understanding! Do not forget, nor turn away from the words of my mouth. Do not forsake her, and she will preserve you; Love her, and she will keep you. Wisdom is the principal thing;
Proverbs 4:5-7 NKJV

THE PURSUIT

What areas of your life do you need to pursue wisdom for?

_____

_____

_____

_____

_____

_____

_____

_____

_____

_____

_____

_____

_____

_____

_____

_____

_____

_____

_____

_____

_____

_____

_____

_____

_____

_____

_____

_____

_____

_____

Reflections

Today I am speaking these words over my life:

Your Word is a lamp to my feet and a light to my path.*

I will embrace wisdom that is from above because it is first pure, then peaceable, gentle, willing to yield, full of mercy and good fruits, without partiality and without hypocrisy.**

*Psalms 119:105   **James 3:17

DAY 7

Worldly Wisdom vs Godly Wisdom

THREE KINDS OF WISDOM

WISDOM FOR TODAY

But now in Christ Jesus you who once were far off have been brought near by the blood of Christ. Ephesians 2:13

There are many wise sayings in the Word of God. List five of your favorites.

_____

_____

_____

_____

_____

_____

On a scale of 1 to 10, how wise were you before you became a Christian? Using the same scale, how wise are you now? What caused the change? List three things you can do to get to 10.

_____

_____

_____

_____

_____

_____

WORLDLY WISDOM VS GODLY WISDOM

God has provided us with many words of wisdom
in the Bible. These are for our protection. Some warnings
take the form of contrast statements, where wisdom gives
us two choices along with the consequences of each choice.
Others take the more aggressive approach, saying "Do not..."
A faithful and wise person can be depended upon to heed
the warnings, to obey even the negatives.

One of the Bible's strongest exhortations and
warnings is found in Proverbs 3:5-8:

> *Trust in the LORD with all your heart, and lean not on
> your own understanding; in all your ways acknowledge
> Him, and He shall direct your paths. Do not be wise in
> your own eyes; fear the LORD and depart from evil. It
> will be health to your flesh, and strength to your bones.*

Our own understanding is too limited; we see things
from our own perspective, out of our experience. God sees
the "big picture," from beginning to end. He is the ultimate
source of wisdom.

Recently, I had an opportunity to attend a very special
meeting in which I was in a leadership capacity with 24 other
people. A devoted woman of prayer who had a reputation
as a great intercessor approached me and explained that
she had a word of knowledge for me. She told me to keep
quiet—don't say anything unless God told me to speak and
then only speak exactly what the Holy Spirit told me to say.
It really shook me and I was so cautious not to speak during

that meeting. I didn't say anything until I knew I was following the leading of the Holy Spirit. And then what I did speak really ushered in a miracle.

It is folly to proceed in our own wisdom when God, in all His omnipotence, desires to guide us and give us wisdom for every action. Pride causes man to lean on his own wisdom instead of God's.

> *Do you see a man wise in his own eyes? There is more hope for a fool than for him.* Proverbs 26:12

If we think we are wise by the standards of our present age, we need to get back to the Word and compare our wisdom with it. The Word may look like foolishness to the world, but it is power—it is the life-changing force. The world's wisdom is destined to be destroyed. That's why it's imperative that we depend on God's wisdom! His Word, not our own understanding or the world's standard of wisdom, is going to put us over! Going our own way is hopeless.

> *Let no one deceive himself. If anyone among you seems to be wise in this age, let him become a fool that he may become wise. For the wisdom of this world is foolishness with God. For it is written, "He catches the wise in their own craftiness"; and again, "The LORD knows the thoughts of the wise, that they are futile."* 1 Corinthians 3:18-20

WORLDLY WISDOM VS GODLY WISDOM

When was the last time you took matters into your own hands in resolving a relationship, financial, or health problem? What did you do?

_____

_____

_____

_____

_____

_____

_____

_____

_____

_____

_____

_____

_____

_____

_____

_____

_____

_____

_____

_____

_____

_____

Reflections

Today I am speaking these words over my life:

Because I have been chosen by God, I have a heart filled with wisdom, compassion, kindness, humility, gentleness, forgiveness, and patience.*

I am always ready to learn more and listen to God's wisdom.**

_____
_____
_____
_____
_____
_____
_____
_____
_____
_____
_____
_____
_____
_____
_____
_____
_____
_____

*Colossians 3:12-13   **Philippians 3:14

DAY 8

Wisdom for Prosperity

FINANCIAL WISDOM

Wisdom for Today

But seek first his kingdom and his righteousness, and all these things will be given to you as well. Therefore do not worry about tomorrow, for tomorrow will worry about itself. Each day has enough trouble of its own.
Matthew 6:28 NIV

What do you think it means to have your soul prosper?

_____
_____
_____
_____
_____
_____
_____

What specific ways would you like your soul to prosper?

_____
_____
_____
_____
_____
_____
_____
_____

WISDOM FOR PROSPERITY

The wisdom of God is for every area of your life—including your finances. In 3 John 2, Jesus said, *"Beloved, I pray that you may prosper in all things and be in health, just as your soul prospers."* That is *Sophia* wisdom. That's God's big picture for you. God wants YOU to prosper. He has given you the wisdom to prosper, the *Phronesis* wisdom:

> *Bring all the tithes into the storehouse so there will be enough food in my Temple. If you do,"* says the LORD almighty, *"I will open the windows of heaven for you. I will pour out a blessing so great you won't have enough room to take it in! Try it! Let me prove it to you!* Malachi 3:10 NLT

If you will operate according to God's wisdom, He will bless you more than you could ever imagine. His ways are different than ours. He may ask you to give something that is out of the ordinary. Just do what he tells you to do.

A woman shared with me about how God used her obedience and fur coat to bless her and her husband in a huge way. On the way to the airport to attend a family reunion in Mexico, they witnessed to the man who was driving them and he accepted Jesus as savior. Then the Lord told the woman to give him her coat for his wife. She was wearing a new fur she had just purchased for $500, and she thought, *"This can't be the Lord telling me to do this. My coat probably isn't even the right size for his wife."*

FINANCIAL WISDOM

So she asked the man what size coat his wife wore. His answer was "10"—the exact size of her coat. Right then she knew it was God telling her to do this so she took it off and gave it to him.

While at their family reunion, one of her relatives asked how much she and her husband owed on their house. When she asked why he wanted to know, he replied "because God told me I am to pay off your house mortgage for you." That $500 seed and this woman's obedience to the Lord's prompting turned into a debt free home for this couple.

Has God ever told you to sow a personal item? What were the circumstances?

_____

_____

_____

_____

_____

_____

_____

_____

_____

_____

_____

_____

_____

Reflections

Today I am speaking these words over my life:

I will prosper in all things and be in health, just as my soul prospers.*

I return to the Lord and obey His voice and the Lord my God will make me abundantly prosperous in all the work of my hand, in everything. For the Lord takes delight in prospering me.**

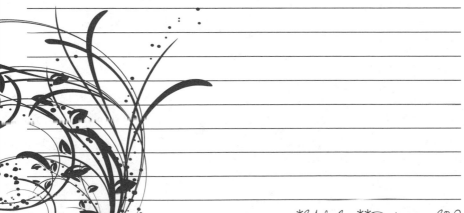

*3 John 2   **Deuteronomy 30:9

Reflections

FINANCIAL WISDOM

DAY 9

No Seed . . . No Harvest

Financial Wisdom

Wisdom for Today

Now he who supplies seed to the sower and bread for food will also supply and increase your store of seed and will enlarge the harvest of your righteousness.
2 Corinthians 9:10

Why do you think God wants us to be givers?

_____

_____

_____

_____

_____

_____

_____

_____

_____

_____

_____

_____

_____

_____

_____

_____

_____

_____

_____

No seed. . .No Harvest

When we look at wisdom for prosperity, we have to start with Genesis and see how God created the earth. The earth began with a seed. He said seed time and harvest will never end. We see that there was no continuance of anything without seed. Seeds are God's building blocks. So without seed there can never be a harvest. When you look at how God handled problems in the Bible, you see He used a seed.

When Adam and Eve sinned, how did God respond? God said the seed of the virgin-born Christ would absolutely destroy the works of the devil. Our redemption started with a Seed. If we want a harvest, there has to be a seed. In Genesis 1 and 2 "God created." However, it never said He created the garden. It said He *planted* the garden. God sowed seed for His creation, Adam and Eve. He sowed a seed to produce a beautiful place for Adam and Eve to live.

We all know the story of how Adam and Eve fell and had to leave the garden. Then Eve gave birth to Cain and Abel. Abel was the righteous seed who brought a blood sacrifice and was accepted by God. Cain did not bring a blood sacrifice and was rejected by God. Cain then rose up and killed Abel. It looked like the devil destroyed the seed, but God knew how to bring forth a replacement seed, and Eve gave birth to Seth.

I learned the concept of "No Seed...No Harvest" early in my ministry. In the beginning, when I first began to travel, I was invited to a large church on the east coast.

FINANCIAL WISDOM

I was so excited about the invitation. The pastor received an offering for me which I was so thankful for. At the time my radio ministry was quite small, and I needed the funds to help with that.

At the end of the night, the pastor said he would mail me a check from the offering. However, he never mailed the check. When I called and told them we never received the check, we were assured that the check was coming. Still no check came, so I called again and wrote a letter to the pastor. Well, I never did get the check from this church and, needless to say, I was very upset. I was bitter toward this pastor. I felt like this money had been stolen from me. Then the Lord dealt with me. God said I should give it to Him, release my bitterness and anger, and adjust my attitude. Then, He said, I would receive a harvest from it. And I did. My radio program grew to 488 stations and all our bills were paid. To this day I take bitterness, sow a seed of forgiveness, and watch God bring a harvest that is well beyond my imagination.

Do you feel like your seed has been destroyed or forgotten? What do you think God could use as a replacement seed?

_____

_____

_____

_____

_____

Reflections

Today I am speaking these words over my life:

Because I give it will be given to me:
good measure, pressed down, shaken together,
and running over... For with the same measure that I give,
it will be measured back to me.*

Because I faithfully till my land, I have plenty of food.**

_____

_____

_____

_____

_____

_____

_____

_____

_____

_____

_____

_____

_____

_____

*Luke 6:38   **Proverbs 28:19

Reflections

DAY 10

Obedience is the Seed

FINANCIAL WISDOM

Wisdom for Today

*Whatever you do, work at it with all your heart,
as working for the Lord, not for men...A faithful man
will be richly blessed...*
Colossians 3:23, Proverbs 28:20

Who or what have you put first in your life? Is it your
relationships, your new car, your career?

_____

_____

_____

_____

_____

_____

_____

How can you reestablish order?

_____

_____

_____

_____

_____

_____

_____

OBEDIENCE IS THE SEED

The key to a successful seed is obedience. Obedience to God is the greatest seed we can sow. God's seed is always going to produce something good, so your obedience to God's Word—the seed—is actually *Phronesis* wisdom. It's what's going to bring a harvest in your life.

Noah is a great example of this. God told Noah to build an ark. It took him 120 years to build the ark and the Bible says that all the time he was building it, he was preaching. People thought he was crazy. But his obedience was his seed. You can't disobey God and expect a big harvest. So Noah continued to build the ark. When it was completed, Noah loaded his family, all the animals, food, and SEED into it. Something very interesting about the layout of the ark is that there was only one door and one window. The window was at the very top, so that all Noah and his family could see was the sky. If there had been windows all around, they would have seen the terrible devastation the flood wrought. But God planned it so the only direction they could look was up!

Noah knew they would need seed for the new world...grain seed and animal seed. When the water receded, the first thing Noah did was build an altar. He had seven clean animals to offer as a sacrifice to God. This was more seed! And from Noah's obedience with the seed, God gave him a beautiful promise.

Financial Wisdom

If you want to prosper like Noah, you've got to keep looking up and keep sowing your seed.

A woman was in one of our services where a missions offering was taken. All she had was $10 to last her 3 days until her next paycheck. God told her to put the $10 in the offering. She gave in joy knowing there was going to be a harvest from that seed. The very next day someone gave her $100 in an envelope. If she had not sown that $10—all she had in her hand, she would not have reaped the blessing of the $100. Obedience is the key to your harvest.

On a scale from 1-10, how would you rate your obedience to God? Why?

_____

_____

_____

_____

_____

_____

_____

_____

_____

_____

_____

_____

_____

Reflections

Today I am speaking these words over my life:

I love the Father and I follow his leading.
He loves me and will show Himself to me.*

I will seek first His righteousness and He will take care of
everything else.**

_____

_____

_____

_____

_____

_____

_____

_____

_____

_____

_____

_____

_____

_____

_____

_____

*John 14: 15, 21   **Matthew 6:33

Reflections

DAY 11

The Power of the Tithe

Financial Wisdom

Wisdom for Today

...God will meet all your needs according to
his glorious riches in Christ Jesus.
Philippians 4:19 NIV

There are times in all of our lives when we have seen God
meet our needs in a way we never expected. Describe one
of those times from your life. What happened? How did He
meet your need?

_____

_____

_____

_____

_____

_____

_____

_____

_____

_____

_____

_____

_____

_____

_____

_____

_____

THE POWER OF THE TITHE

Tithing is powerful and important. It is the power for prosperity. In Malachi 3:10 God promises if you tithe, you will have such blessing that you will not have enough room to contain it. He will rebuke the devourer and He will open the windows of heaven if you are a tither. This is the power of the tithe.

I started tithing when I was 11 years old. I was in the sixth grade. One day my mother told me that because money was so tight for our family, I needed to start buying my own clothes. That's when I began babysitting and selling apples from our farm in Pennsylvania. Soon thereafter, my mother taught me the importance of tithing. So every Sunday I would tithe from the money I had made that week.

When I was 16 years old, I told my father I wanted to go to college. He told me I would have to get scholarships and work to pay for it myself. I worked and continued to tithe all through college. When I graduated, I had no loans to pay off or any other debt to speak of. If you don't tithe, you don't have seed for the harvest.

The first tither is found in Genesis 14:17. Abraham tithes to Melchizadek, a priest of God Most High, who in turn speaks a tremendous blessing over Abraham:

> ...Blessed be Abram by God Most High, Creator of heaven and earth. And blessed be God Most High, who delivered your enemies into your hand. Then Abram gave him a tenth of everything.
> Genesis 14: 19-20 NIV

FINANCIAL WISDOM

Abraham was obedient and God blessed him as a result. When you tithe, doors of blessing open.

> Genesis 15:1 states *...the Lord came to Abram in a vision, saying, "Do not be afraid, Abram. I am your shield, your exceedingly great reward."*

Abraham believed God and counted on Him for his righteousness and blessing. A tither can trust God wherever he is. In times of drought or in times of flood, he has tithe seed working for him to bring a harvest. It may come in a very unique way; we don't know how God will bring it, but God promises it.

Tithing takes obedience and faith. Which do you find more challenging: Being obedient to God with your tithe or having faith that He will meet your needs each month as you tithe? Why?

_____

_____

_____

_____

_____

_____

_____

Reflections

Today I am speaking these words over my life:

I know that the purpose of tithing is to teach me
to put God first in my life—everyday.*

I will not withhold good when it is in my power to do good.
I will not send my neighbor away empty handed when I can
bless him today.**

_____

_____

_____

_____

_____

_____

_____

_____

_____

_____

_____

_____

_____

_____

_____

_____

*Deuteronomy 14:23   **Proverbs 3:27 28

Reflections

DAY 12

Sow Your Tithe — Rebuke the Devourer

FINANCIAL WISDOM

Wisdom for Today

Each man should give what he has decided in his heart to give, not reluctantly or under compulsion, for God loves a cheerful giver. 2 Corinthians 9:8

Do you consider yourself a cheerful giver? Why?

_____

_____

_____

_____

_____

_____

_____

Give an example of a time you gave cheerfully.

_____

_____

_____

_____

_____

_____

_____

Sow Your Tithe—Rebuke the Devourer

Tithing. Do you believe it will work for you or do you uproot it with your mouth?

God gave Abraham his harvest, Isaac. But then He asked him to plant more seed...to sacrifice his harvest, his son.

> *Then God said, "Take your son, your only son, Isaac, whom you love, and go to the region of Moriah. Sacrifice him there as a burnt offering on one of the mountains I will tell you about."* Genesis 22:2 NIV

Abraham couldn't believe God was asking him to do this. But he obeyed and prepared to offer his greatest sacrifice...his greatest act of obedience.

And Abraham *did not* uproot his tithe with his mouth. He spoke faith and life into his tithe...his sacrifice.

> *He said to his servants, "Stay here with the donkey while I and the boy go over there. We will worship and then we will come back to you."* Genesis 22:5 NIV

Because Abraham was a tither and willing to give up his most precious seed, God made a provision with a ram in the thicket.

> *So Abraham called that place The LORD Will Provide. And to this day it is said, "On the mountain of the LORD it will be provided."* Genesis 22:14 NIV

FINANCIAL WISDOM

God is the God who sees ahead and makes a provision. Then the angel of the Lord spoke to Abraham and told him,

I swear by myself, declares the LORD, that because you have done this and have not withheld your son, your only son, I will surely bless you and make your descendants as numerous as the stars in the sky and as the sand on the seashore. Your descendants will take possession of the cities of their enemies, and through your offspring all nations on earth will be blessed, because you have obeyed me. Genesis 22:16-18

The power of the seed and how God uses it is so wonderful. Tithing is power and God uses that power to be our shield and our exceeding great reward. We must put faith in it, not just go through the motions, but put faith in it and speak over our seed, water it with our mouths.

One of our partners, who is also a pastor, shared with us how he was in desperate need of a new car. For several years he had a practice of giving $100 bills to single moms to help with their daily expenses. One day he decided it was time to really call in his harvest. He started to speak the promises of God over his seed. That very week he received three $100 bills anonymously. Shortly thereafter, he received 15—$100 bills out of the blue. Then, for Christmas, someone gave him three cashier's checks totaling $27,000 for him to buy a new car! He also received over $1,500 from people thanking him for his service over the years. His faithfulness in planting the seed and watering it paid off in a great way!

Have you ever lost your blessing because your mouth was speaking contrary to what you prayed or what the Word says? What could you have done differently?

_____
_____
_____
_____
_____
_____
_____
_____
_____
_____
_____
_____
_____
_____
_____
_____
_____
_____

Reflections

Today I am speaking these words over my life:

I have given to God my tithes and offerings and they are in God's hands as seeds of my faith. My seeds of time, service, money, and ministry are sown and God is growing them invisibly and absolutely. God is changing my seedtime into harvest time. God is rebuking the devourer for my sake.*

I will not lay up treasures for myself on this earth but I choose to lay up treasures in heaven where it can not be destroyed or stolen.**

*Malachi 3:10-12   **Matthew 6:19,20

DAY 13

Tithing + Offering=Harvest

Financial Wisdom

Wisdom for Today

Give and it will be given to you: good measure, pressed down, shaken together, and running over... For with the same measure that you use, it will be measured back to you.
Luke 6:38

Think about the concept "with the same measure that you use, it will be measured to you." Where do you see this principle in your own life?

_____

_____

_____

_____

_____

_____

_____

_____

_____

_____

_____

_____

_____

_____

_____

_____

TITHING + OFFERING = HARVEST

Tithing and offering have harvest attached to them but often in different ways.   The tithe rebukes the devourer and opens the windows of heaven but the offering causes men to give.

Here is a great example of God's *Sophia* wisdom and how He sees the big picture of Elijah's life.

In 1 Kings 17 Elijah received a word from the Lord saying that there was going to be a drought and famine in the land.

> *Then the word of the LORD came to Elijah: "Leave here, turn eastward and hide in the Kerith Ravine, east of the Jordan. You will drink from the brook, and I have ordered the ravens to feed you there."*
> 1Kings 17:2 NIV

After a while, the brook dried up but God did not leave Elijah in trouble.

> *Go at once to Zaraphath of Sidon and stay there. I have commanded a widow in that place to supply you with food.* I Kings 17:9

When Elijah arrived and found the widow, he asked her for a drink of water and some bread. She told him that she only has enough flour and oil to make one more cake for her and her son and then there would be nothing left and they would surely die.

FINANCIAL WISDOM

Elijah said to her "Don't be afraid. Go home and do as you have said. But first make a small cake of bread for me from what you have and bring it to me, and then make something for yourself and your son. For this is what the LORD, the God of Israel says: 'The jar of flour will not be used up and the jug of oil will not run dry until the day the LORD gives rain on the land.'"
1 Kings 17:14 NIV

God was asking this woman to take the small seed she had in her hand—her offering—and sow it. True to His Word, the widow woman's flour and oil supply did not dry up and later her son did not die because of Elijah's presence.

Many years ago we set aside $60,000.00 for outreaches in China. I have been there 29 times and we have always sowed into that country. Well, we knew a pastor in Kenya who was building a Bible school and the Lord told us to give him $55,000.00. I said, "Lord, that is all we have and it is our seed for China. What will we do for China if we give the money to this pastor in Kenya?" But we knew this was from God so we gave the money to Kenya for the Bible school.

Shortly after we gave the money, a man called me from Africa asking how much our China budget was for the year. I told him $60,000.00. He said that his business felt led to sow $60,000.00 into our ministry for China and believe me...I definitely felt led to receive it! We sowed into Africa and reaped from Africa for China! The power of God is so awesome!

Has God been nudging you to give more offerings? What outreaches has He placed on your heart?

_____

_____

_____

_____

_____

_____

_____

_____

_____

_____

_____

_____

_____

_____

_____

_____

_____

_____

_____

_____

_____

_____

Reflections

Today I am speaking these words over my life:

I will give my offerings and rejoice in how God uses "men" to bless me. God will meet my needs through someone else's generosity.*

I know that it is a privilege to give and that riches and honor come from God.**

_____

_____

_____

_____

_____

_____

_____

_____

_____

_____

_____

_____

_____

_____

_____

*Luke 6:38   **1 Cronicles 29:12-18

DAY 14

Supernatural Provision

FINANCIAL WISDOM

Wisdom for Today

For it is from God alone that you have your life through Christ Jesus. He showed us God's plan of salvation; he was the one who made us acceptable to God; he made us pure and holy and gave himself to purchase our salvation. ..."If anyone is going to boast, let him boast only of what the Lord has done."
1 Corinthians 1:30-31 TLB

List some times of "famine or drought" in your life where you know God provided for you. How did He do it?

_____

_____

_____

_____

_____

_____

In what ways did it affect your life?

_____

_____

_____

_____

_____

_____

_____

SUPERNATURAL PROVISION

Genesis 22 is the first chapter in the Bible where the name Jehovah Jireh appears after The Lord showed Himself to Abraham on the basis of meeting his needs.

When you discover how this name applies to you, you will know that Jehovah Jireh not only met Abraham's needs, but He also desires to meet your needs. Remember, Jehovah is the eternal changeless One Who reveals His ways to you. By calling Himself Jehovah Jireh, He is saying, *"I do not change—My ways do not change; therefore, I desire to meet your needs, just as I met the needs of the children of Israel in their exodus from Egypt."*

God has seen ahead and made a provision to fill your need. There is not one trial or problem that you may be encountering that God has not already seen and made provision to take care of. Why? Because he is your Jehovah Jireh, just as he was Abraham's Jehovah Jireh. He knows all things. He already knows what you will encounter in your life, and He has a provision for you to handle it.

Just recently God opened the doors for us to host a Ministry Training School for pastors and leaders in Cairo, Egypt. Initially we anticipated just over 2000 pastors and leaders. Days before the event, that number grew to 3500, and we prepared for exactly that number. But, in God's perfect plan and to our great surprise, nearly 5000 showed up for the meeting!

Financial Wisdom

At these events, we provide a meal to bless these great servants of the Lord. However, like many places in the world, Cairo has been experiencing food shortages, widespread hunger, and riots had occurred just a few days before we arrived.

This was our dilemma: we had a huge and hungry crowd who wanted to learn from Jesus—yet a shortage of food. Sound familiar? (See John 6:1-13).

Amazingly, just as God multiplied the loaves and fish to feed the five thousand that day long ago—He miraculously multiplied our simple boxed lunches to feed our five thousand in Cairo!

Exactly 3500 tickets for boxed lunches were counted and handed out to attendees. Our ministry team counted out exactly 3500 boxed lunches. The boxes are important because they allowed us to easily count exactly how God multiplied the food.

After each of the tickets for the boxed lunches had been collected, with many hungry people still waiting for food, the staff counted 1200 more boxes! Once those boxes had been handed out, the staff counted again and miraculously another 1200 boxes were there. That is a total of 2400 more boxes than were delivered!

By the end of the day there were so many extra boxes that we were able to bless security guards, police, neighborhood kids and the homeless with boxed lunches. After years of praying and believing God, we experienced a mathematically-verifiable Miracle of Multiplication!

Supernatural Provision

The provision is there. When we chose to serve the Lord,
all the resources of heaven became available. Christ paid
the price for those things that money can never purchase:
health, healing, safety, financial provision, as well as
righteousness, wisdom, peace, joy, and eternal life. Through
obedience to God and faith in His Word, we have all things
that pertain to the natural, as well as the spiritual life.

What obstacles are you facing right now that require you to
see God as your Jehovah Jireh?

_____

_____

_____

_____

_____

_____

_____

_____

_____

_____

_____

_____

_____

_____

_____

_____

_____

Reflections

Today I am speaking these words over my life:

His divine power has given me everything I need for life and godliness through my knowledge of Him who called me by His own glory and goodness.*

I will abound with blessings because I am a faithful servant of God.**

_____

_____

_____

_____

_____

_____

_____

_____

_____

_____

_____

_____

_____

_____

_____

_____

*2 Peter 1:3   **Proverbs 28:20a

DAY 15

Wisdom for Your Body

WISDOM FOR HEALTH

WISDOM FOR TODAY

Do you not know that your body is a temple of the Holy Spirit, who is in you, whom you have received from God? You are not your own; you were bought at a price. Therefore honor God with your body. 1 Corinthians 6:18-20 NIV

What do you think it means "to honor God with your body"? How do you show "honor" for someone or something?

_____

_____

_____

_____

_____

_____

What do you think you need to do to live up to 1 Corinthians 6:18-20?

_____

_____

_____

_____

_____

_____

_____

WISDOM FOR YOUR BODY

Everyone wants good health. You can't enjoy relationships without good health. You can't enjoy wealth without good health. You can have all your financial needs met, but you won't enjoy it if you don't feel well. It's even hard to enjoy God or spiritual things when your body feels bad.

God has *Sophia* wisdom for your health: He wants us whole—spirit, soul, and body. He doesn't just want you to be spiritually whole; He wants your mind and emotions whole and He wants your body to be whole as well. The Lord is concerned about the health of your body. He created it, and He wants it to be healthy. He says in 1 Corinthians 6:13, *"…The body is…for the Lord; and the Lord for the body"* (ASV).

As Christians, we have all quoted Isaiah 53:5: *"…Because of our sins he was wounded, beaten because of the evil we did. We are healed by the punishment he suffered, made whole by the blows he received"* (TEV). Yes, Jesus took our sicknesses and diseases, but God has still given us wisdom for health.

When Moses died, he basically died in good health. He received the revelation of *Jehovah Rophe*—the Lord our healer—or "the Lord our health." Moses understood that not only did the Lord want him well, He wanted him to stay healthy.

WISDOM FOR HEALTH

And Moses was an hundred and twenty years old when he died: his eye was not dim, nor his natural force abated. Deuteronomy 34:7 KJV

Moses walked in the revelation *"the Lord is for the body and the body is for the Lord."*

We need to get that revelation also. We often think that it's nobody's business but our own what we eat and what we do to our bodies. The fact of the matter is, it's God's business what we eat. I believe we grieve the Holy Spirit when we fail to take good care of God's temple— our bodies.

I love to pray for the sick and I've done it all over the world. It concerns me, however, when I see someone come forward for prayer who is seriously overweight. I pray for them and because of God's grace they're healed. But I know in my spirit that because of their lifestyle they'll allow sickness and disease to drag them back into the same situation.

We can't continue to break all the rules concerning good health and expect to live a healthy life. We can be anointed with oil, have prayer cloths in every pocket, but if we still eat junk food and don't exercise— the chances of getting sick again are astronomical. The sad thing is this: it doesn't have to be that way.

WISDOM FOR YOUR BODY

God has given us one body for this life, and we need to be good stewards. Good stewardship of our bodies means making wise choices, exercising, and eating right.

Do you think you're ready to take responsibility for your own health and well-being? Why or why not?

_____

_____

_____

_____

_____

_____

_____

_____

_____

_____

_____

_____

_____

_____

_____

_____

_____

_____

_____

_____

_____

Reflections

Today I am speaking these words over my life:

The Lord is for my body…and my body is for the Lord.*

I eat and drink to the glory of God.**

*1 Corinthians 6:13   **1 Corinthians 10:31

DAY 16

Food Foibles

WISDOM FOR HEALTH

WISDOM FOR TODAY

*…Whether you eat or drink, or whatever you may do, do all
for the honor and glory of God.*
1 Corinthians 10:31 TAB

Do you think you have a problem with overeating, or eating
the wrong kinds of food? What are some of the reasons
you turn to food to meet needs?

_____

_____

_____

_____

_____

_____

_____

In what ways would you like to change your eating habits
and/or improve your overall health?

_____

_____

_____

_____

_____

_____

FOOD FOIBLES

If you have trouble with food, you are not alone. What was the first thing Adam and Eve got in trouble over? It was food. God told them not to eat from a particular tree.

When the woman saw that the fruit of the tree was good for food and pleasing to the eye, and also desirable for gaining wisdom, she took some and ate it.
Genesis 3:6 NIV

Then she gave it to Adam to eat, and they were banished from the Garden as a result of their disobedience.

Do you remember Belshazzar? Belshazzar, the king of Babylon, threw a big feast one night which turned into a drunken brawl (Daniel 5). He even drank from the holy vessels. Food and drink had dulled his senses and contributed to his fall from power. The writing was on the wall. Judgment fell upon him that night and his kingdom was lost as a result.

What about Esau? One day, he came home from hunting tired and hungry. When he smelled the stew Jacob was cooking, he begged his brother to give him a bowl. Jacob was willing to trade—a bowl for his birthright.

"Look, I'm dying of starvation!" said Esau. "What good is my birthright to me now?" So Jacob insisted, "Well then, swear to me right now that it is mine." So Esau swore an oath, thereby selling all his rights as the

firstborn to his younger brother. Then Jacob gave Esau some bread and lentil stew. Esau ate and drank and went on about his business, indifferent to the fact that he had given up his birthright.
Genesis 25:29-34 NLT

Esau was willing to give up his birthright, the blessing that rightfully belonged to him, for food.

In First Samuel, we read about another man who loved to eat—Eli. Eli and his sons loved fat meat...and his sons would steal the fat from the sacrifices that were offered on the altar. God warned Eli twice to get his sons under control, but Eli just could not give up his eating habits or discipline his sons. He was so overweight that when he heard about the Ark of the Covenant being stolen, he fell backward from his seat, broke his neck, and died *"...for he was old and very fat"* (1 Samuel 4:18 NLT.)

We all have weaknesses when it comes to food, especially around the holidays. I love getting together with friends and family, watching a football game, and enjoying a fabulous dinner together. Have you noticed that all your favorite foods seem to come out at Thanksgiving? And, if you're like most people you'll eat all day even when you're full. Then there are all the leftovers to eat.

FOOD FOIBLES

It's insane what we do to our bodies during the holidays but the good news is that you don't have to be out of control. God's Word has the key. It says in Proverbs 27:7 that *"a satisfied soul loathes the honeycomb, but to a hungry soul every bitter thing is sweet."* The important word is "soul" which is your mind, will, and emotions. If you take care of your mind and emotions you won't be tempted to eat everything in sight. It's when your soul is not satisfied that you're most tempted to overeat. The solution: keep your mind occupied. Stay active and try to have someone to talk to. Sometimes a friend who is an accountability partner will make all the difference.

What are your areas of weakness when it comes to healthy eating? What can you do to address these areas?

_____

_____

_____

_____

_____

_____

_____

_____

_____

Reflections

Today I am speaking these words over my life:

I eat and am satisfied. I do not overeat or desire unhealthy foods or desserts.*

I am free from every bad habit, in Jesus' name. I can do all things through Christ who strengthens me. Greater is He who is in me than he who is in the world.**

_____

_____

_____

_____

_____

_____

_____

_____

_____

_____

_____

_____

_____

_____

_____

_____

_____

*Proverbs 13:25 and Proverbs 23:3
**John 8:36 and John 4:4

DAY 17

Appetite Control

WISDOM FOR HEALTH

WISDOM FOR TODAY

And put a knife to your throat
if you are a man given to appetite. Proverbs 23:2

This seems pretty extreme. What do you think God is trying to reveal to us in this scripture?

_____

_____

_____

_____

_____

_____

_____

_____

_____

_____

_____

_____

_____

_____

_____

_____

_____

_____

_____

_____

APPETITE CONTROL

Do you control your appetite—or does your appetite control you? And if it's the latter—you need *Sophia*, *Phronesis*, and *Sunesis* wisdom in order to help you live a balanced life. For some of us, we need all the wisdom we can get.

God has given us all a natural desire for food. We know that our bodies require food to sustain them. But what happens when this natural desire takes over our lives? What happens when our eating habits begin to impact our health, relationships, and even our finances?

What are some of the main obstacles that negatively impact our eating habits? Here are a few of the culprits.

Laziness

Laziness casts into a deep sleep. And an idle man will suffer hunger. Proverbs 19:15

He who is full loathes honey, but to the hungry even what is bitter tastes sweet. Proverbs 27:7 NIV

Have you ever noticed that when you don't have much to do and you're bored, it's the easiest time to run to the refrigerator and eat—even when you're not hungry? Have you ever noticed that when you're not really busy, you tend to think more about food?

WISDOM FOR HEALTH

Paul wrote in Philippians 4:8

Finally, brothers, whatever is true, whatever is noble, whatever is right, whatever is pure, whatever is lovely, whatever is admirable-if anything is excellent or praiseworthy-think about such things (NIV).

It's good to keep your body and your mind busy. The person whose mind is full and complete is constantly thinking about worthwhile things, making worthwhile plans. People with full souls are not always thinking about sweets or what they're going to eat for dinner; they are too busy filling their minds with more productive things. On the other hand, the hungry soul, or the person whose mind is lazy and undisciplined, always thinks about food. Even bitter things taste good to this person! Keep your body busy; keep your mind busy and full of the Word. Then your eating habits will become pleasing to the Lord.

Emptiness

The righteous have enough to eat, but the wicked are always hungry. Proverbs 13:25-14:1 TEV

You can eat to satisfy your appetite—or go beyond that and stuff yourself! Most of the time, the reason we go beyond satisfying the body is because the food tastes so good. But the Bible gives us these warnings:

> *Do not join those who drink too much wine or gorge themselves on meat....* Proverbs 23:20 NIV

> *It is not good to eat much honey....*
> Proverbs 25:27 NIV

The righteous, those that honor God with their bodies, don't go beyond being satisfied—they stay within their limit.

"Deceptive" foods

> *Do not crave his delicacies, for that food is deceptive.*
> Proverbs 23:3 NIV

Over-indulgence in delicacies, like sweets, can hurt you. They look good, but looks can be deceiving! They may smell good and they taste good, but they are not necessarily good for you. I love fudge and to make matters worse a friend of mine makes the best fudge in the whole world! Every Christmas she brings over a big can filled with fudge. But now I have a plan that keeps me from giving in to my craving. I make a decision BEFOREHAND to ONLY eat three pieces. I can eat all three pieces in one day, three days, or over a two week period. It's my choice how I control the portions. The key to success is that I make the decision and stick with it—no matter what. I've found that it works for other foods too. I've always had a good appetite but this is the best appetite control plan I've ever used. It works for me and I know it'll work for you.

Do you or someone you love have challenges staying away from foods that are not good for you? List three things you can do today to control your appetite?

1. _____

_____

_____

_____

2. _____

_____

_____

_____

3. _____

_____

_____

_____

_____

Reflections

Today I am speaking these words over my life:

I take the sin of lust for food to the cross. I am dead to the sin of overeating and alive unto God.*

I exercise discipline and self-control over my eating habits. I do not overeat.**

_____

_____

_____

_____

_____

_____

_____

_____

_____

_____

_____

_____

_____

_____

_____

_____

*Romans 6:1   **2 Timothy 1:7

Reflections

DAY 18

The Kingdom of God vs. The Kingdom of Food

WISDOM FOR HEALTH

WISDOM FOR TODAY

For the kingdom of God is not a matter of eating and drinking, but of righteousness, peace and joy in the Holy Spirit. Romans 14:17-18 NIV

Ask God to give you an understanding of what Romans 14:17 means. What are some of the insights that you are receiving?

_____

_____

_____

_____

_____

_____

What are some of the things you can do to "seek the kingdom of God and His righteousness" for your health?

_____

_____

_____

_____

_____

_____

_____

THE KINGDOM OF GOD VS. THE KINGDOM OF FOOD

Americans are famous for obsessing about our appearances and especially our weight. God doesn't want us to dwell on whether we're too fat or too skinny. God wants us to take our eyes off our problem and put our eyes on the kingdom of God. As we seek the "kingdom of God and His righteousness," the Bible says *all things will be added unto us* (Matthew 6:33). As we get God's perspective on eating it will help us have the proper attitude about food. Here are 9 things you can do to help you overcome bad eating habits.

1. Keep your mind active—think on the right things. *Laziness casts into deep sleep, and an idle man will suffer hunger.*
   Proverbs 19:15 NASB

2. Eat just to satisfy and ask God for wisdom when to stop. *The righteous have enough to eat, but the wicked are always hungry.*
   Proverbs 13:25-14:1 TEV

3. Watch your intake of meats and sweets.
   Do not crave his delicacies, for that food is deceptive.
   Proverbs 23:3 NIV
   Do not join those who drink too much wine or gorge themselves on meat....
   Proverbs 23:20 NIV

WISDOM FOR HEALTH

4. Eat to glorify God.
   *…Whether you eat or drink, or whatever you may
   do, do all for the honor and glory of God.*
   1 Corinthians 10:31 TAB

5. Take your bad eating habits to the cross and
   reckon them dead.
   *In the same way, count yourselves dead to sin but
   alive to God in Christ Jesus.*
   Romans 6:11 NIV

6. Pray in the Spirit before you sit down to eat.
   *In the same way, the Spirit helps us in
   our weakness.*
   Romans 8:26 NIV

7. Speak the right words over your food before you eat.
   *From the fruit of his mouth a man's stomach is
   filled; with the harvest from his lips he is satisfied.*
   Proverbs 18:20 NIV

8. Don't eat when you are depressed.
   *All the days of the afflicted are bad, But a cheerful
   heart has a continual feast.*
   Proverbs 15:15 NASU

9. Pray God's Word over your food.
   For everything created by God is good, and nothing is to be rejected if it is received with gratitude; for it is sanctified by means of the word of God and prayer.
   1 Timothy 4:4-5 NASU

Do you pray over your food before you eat? Sometimes I think we do it because that's what we're taught in Sunday school or by our parents—it's simply what Christians do. But it's Godly wisdom to pray over every meal in order to sanctify your food.

I remember once when I was in Ethiopia I was served food that I knew was unclean. I was in a quandary, however, because I didn't want to insult my host. So I prayed over my food believing by faith that it was now sanctified and that nothing I ate would harm me. I didn't get sick. It's happened to me in other places around the world also and each time God's sanctifying power kept me healthy. He can do the same for you.

Wisdom for Health

There's a battle going on in our lives 24/7 between our flesh and our spirit. The condition of our physical health is often an indicator of who's winning the battle. What can you do to ensure that you're Spirit-led when it comes to your health?

_____

_____

_____

_____

_____

_____

_____

_____

_____

_____

_____

_____

_____

_____

_____

_____

_____

_____

_____

_____

_____

_____

Reflections

Today I am speaking these words over my life:

I seek the kingdom of God, which is righteousness, peace and joy in the Holy Spirit.*

I am filled with the Spirit and do not seek to follow the lusts of the flesh.**

_____

_____

_____

_____

_____

_____

_____

_____

_____

_____

_____

_____

_____

_____

_____

_____

_____

_____

_____

*Romans 14:17   **Romans 8:5

Reflections

DAY 19

Life in the Fast Lane

WISDOM FOR HEALTH

WISDOM FOR TODAY

"Go, gather all the Jews who are present in Shushan, and fast for me; neither eat nor drink for three days, night or day. My maids and I will fast likewise. And so I will go to the king, which is against the law; and if I perish, I perish!"
Esther 4:16 NKJV

When was the last time you went on a fast? How long did you fast?

_____

_____

_____

_____

_____

_____

_____

What was your reason for fasting?

_____

_____

_____

_____

_____

_____

_____

Life in the Fast Lane

There is one sure thing you can do that will help you immensely in the food and health battle. It's fasting. It's one of the most powerful ways to improve your health, but it's also one of the ways that's most misunderstood and least practiced in the body of Christ. Fasting is more than just not eating.

It may seem ironic that "fasting" would be offered as a way to help you gain control of your eating habits. But before discounting this suggestion as not for you, think about trying it "in a small way" to begin with. Think in terms of fasting a meal or a certain type of food during a meal, for one day. Pray for God's grace and offer this small sacrifice to Him. You will be surprised by the benefits of fasting, combined with prayer. You really just have to try it to be convinced of the power it will bring into your life. There's no better way to crucify the flesh and exalt your spirit than by prayer and fasting. Fasting will bring health to your spirit, soul, and body!

A member of my staff was informed by an oncologist (a doctor specializing in cancer treatment) that a MRI and CAT scan revealed a tumor on his kidney. The diagnosis was probable malignancy but she decided to refer him to an urologist with expertise in the treatment of kidney diseases. Shortly thereafter, the Lord called this man to fast. Although he was experienced in fasting, he received no specific instructions from the Holy Spirit about goals or length of the fast. He simply obeyed and began a fast of juice and water.

The urologist that examined the MRI and CAT scan results agreed that there was a 95% probability that the tumor was malignant. He scheduled further tests to determine the best surgical procedure. The new series of tests were administered on day 27 of the fast. When the urologist saw the lab results he simply said, "You're the luckiest man alive." He downloaded onto his computer all the images of the kidney taken throughout the testing process. The tumor had completely disappeared sometime during the third week of the fast!

When the man was driving home from the doctor's office the Lord revealed to him that it was his obedience to the Holy Spirit's leading coupled with the power of prayer and fasting that had released his miracle healing.

Life in the Fast Lane

3 Tips for Praying and Fasting

1. As you think about fasting, begin by committing your fast to the Lord. Here's a prayer that can help you.

   Heavenly Father, I commit this fast to You. I ask for Your grace, strength, and guidance during this time. It's my desire to walk in health and wholeness. I confess I need more self-control, wisdom, and discipline over my eating habits. Help me in this fast, and I believe as I do so, yokes and bondages will be broken off my life, in Jesus' name. Amen.

2. Ask the Lord to help you choose what to fast and for how long. Remember this is not a "religious exercise," so you don't need to be hard on yourself. Offer what you think you can do to the Lord, and He will multiply it for your benefit.

3. Keep a daily journal. You will wish you did this afterwards if you have not done this before. Express your feelings about the fast, what you are believing will happen, what scriptures you are meditating on, what spiritual changes you are noticing, etc.

WISDOM FOR HEALTH

Where could you get Phronesis "how to" or Sunesis
"networking" wisdom for your next fast? List any
strongholds you would like to see broken the next time
you fast.

_____

_____

_____

_____

_____

_____

_____

_____

_____

_____

_____

_____

_____

_____

_____

_____

_____

_____

_____

_____

_____

_____

_____

Reflections

Today I am speaking these words over my life:

As I fast and pray, I believe I am being set free from a desire for the wrong kinds of food. I believe I am gaining self-discipline.*

I submit to God and resist the enemy, and the enemy flees from me.**

_____

_____

_____

_____

_____

_____

_____

_____

_____

_____

_____

_____

_____

_____

*John 8:36 NIV   **James 4:7

Reflections

DAY 20

Quality of Life

WISDOM FOR HEALTH

WISDOM FOR TODAY

He [David] *died at a good old age, having enjoyed long life, wealth, and honor.*
I Chronicles 29:28 NIV

Everyday we make choices that impact our quality of life. Make a list of the positive and negative choices that have made the most dramatic impact on your life. What pattern did you notice?

QUALITY OF LIFE

How do you measure a high level quality of life? Some people would try to convince you that money is the best measuring stick. Others might say that it's all about family; a wonderful marriage with great children. But I don't think that's where it starts. I believe a quality life starts with a decision to be healthy in your body. It's God's *Sophia* wisdom for our lives. He wants us to be good stewards of our body.

I remember when I was growing up I was not a good athlete. As a matter of fact when it was time to choose sides for a ballgame, I was always the last one picked—and I didn't try to overcome or change it. But when I got to my mid-forties, I noticed that my metabolism was changing. I started to gain weight and I noticed the overall quality of my health began to be affected. I made a decision that I was not going to let my body go downhill. I was going to make a change and get my body in line with God's *Sophia* wisdom for my life—that I would lead a long and fruitful life.

The choice was mine! Now I needed Phronesis wisdom to know how to carry it out. During that time, I spent some time with my aunt who was undergoing physical therapy. During these therapy sessions, I witnessed a group of older people who went through an amazing transformation. In the beginning, their physical condition was extremely poor. Many couldn't get out of their wheelchairs, and they looked emotionally drained and defeated. However, after they started therapy, their bodies began to respond to the exercise. After only 10 days, they began to socialize more and many got out of their wheelchairs. As I talked to some of them, it seemed that even their memory had improved.

I realized then and there how dramatically we could improve the quality of our lives, just by being physically active. In the beginning, I simply started by taking long walks. As I became more and more fit, I added other exercises to my lifestyle. That was God's *Phronesis* wisdom for me. My husband and members of our staff walked with me. That was God's *Sunesis* wisdom working in my life.

When I reached my sixties, my body began to change again. I knew I needed more *Phronesis* wisdom to maintain a high quality of life. So, I began to read articles on exercise for mature adults. I learned that you don't have to spend hundreds of dollars to join a fancy health club. There are a lot of community centers with heath facilities that are free, and there are exercise programs on television almost every day. Remember, the decision to lead a quality life begins with a simple decision—and God has the *Phronesis* and *Sunesis* wisdom to insure that your life will be healthier and happier as a result.

QUALITY OF LIFE

What are five things that you could do on a consistent basis to improve the quality of your life? What are the biggest challenges you face? Who's the best person in your life that can be part of God's *Sunesis* wisdom for you?

_____

_____

_____

_____

_____

_____

_____

_____

_____

_____

_____

_____

_____

_____

_____

_____

_____

_____

_____

_____

_____

_____

_____

_____

_____

Reflections

Today I am speaking these words over my life:

My body will glow with health, and my very bones will vibrate with life!*

The law of the spirit of life in Christ Jesus has set me free from the law of sin and death.**

_____

_____

_____

_____

_____

_____

_____

_____

_____

_____

_____

_____

_____

_____

_____

_____

_____

_____

*Proverbs 3:8   **Romans 8:2

DAY 21

3 kinds of Exercise

WISDOM FOR HEALTH

WISDOM FOR TODAY

...I discipline my body like an athlete, training it to do what it should. 1 Corinthians 9:27 NLT

How does an athlete discipline his body?

_____

_____

_____

_____

_____

_____

_____

_____

Do you exercise regularly? What is your exercise routine?

_____

_____

_____

_____

_____

_____

_____

_____

3 KINDS OF EXERCISE

Okay, you've decided that it's time to take better care of your body. That's *Sophia* "big picture" wisdom. Taking into account your schedule and physical condition, where are you going to get the *Phronesis* "practical" wisdom to achieve your goals?

I have discovered that not only did God give us three kinds of wisdom—He also gave us three kinds of exercise to keep our bodies strong and healthy. We need all three kinds of wisdom and all three kinds of exercise, because we have different kinds of muscle groups that need different types of exercise.

Most personal trainers agree our bodies benefit greatly when exposed to all three kinds of exercise. It's important to do 1) some kind of stretching or flexibility development, which also builds strength; 2) cardiovascular exercise for the heart and circulation, and finally 3) weight training for muscle and bone strength.

Exercise is important because it improves memory and stimulates brain activity. But probably most important— excess weight and little or no physical activity can lead to high cholesterol, high blood pressure, and diabetes. I discovered that I had high cholesterol when I was in my fifties. This was a real concern for me because my family had a history of heart trouble. So I made a decision to increase my cardiovascular exercise. That was *Phronesis* wisdom operating in my life. Want to know what happened? My cholesterol began to go down.

WISDOM FOR HEALTH

Shortly thereafter, I met a woman who was God's *Sunesis* wisdom for me. She was a personal trainer and she took me under her wing. She introduced me to Pilates which improved my flexibility and strength. She taught me how to do stretching with an exercise band. It's so easy to use. I can stand, sit, or lie down and do exercises with it. It stretches the body and makes you more agile. Now, I carry my Pilates band with me whenever I travel. No matter how busy my schedule is, I have no excuses not to exercise because my Pilates band is as close as my suitcase.

That brings me to a very important point. Nowhere is Sunesis wisdom more important than when exercising. An exercise partner can mean the difference between success and failure. When you network with a friend during your exercise program you've got someone to exhort you and keep you working toward your goal—that's *Sophia* wisdom, *Phronesis*, and *Sunesis* wisdom working together.

When it comes to exercise—"a little" every day goes a long way. The older you get, the more you need to exercise your body. Every time you exercise, you take your body to a new level. Think about this. Pray about this. Ask God to help you structure an exercise program. There's an exercise program for every lifestyle and physical condition. All of us can do something!

A healthy and strong body starts with a commitment to exercise. Ask God to give you the self-discipline you need. Pray for Him to show you how to combine these three types of exercise in a way that fits into your lifestyle. You will notice a definite improvement in your health if you do!

3 KINDS OF EXERCISE

Consider taking time right now to ask God to help you exercise and to trust Christ to give you the strength and discipline that you need.

Where can you get the *Sophia*, *Phronesis*, and *Sunesis* wisdom you need to be successful in your exercise program?

_____

_____

_____

_____

_____

_____

_____

_____

_____

_____

_____

_____

_____

_____

_____

_____

_____

_____

_____

_____

_____

_____

_____

Reflections

Today I am speaking these words over my life:

I can do all things because Christ gives me the strength.*

Daily God bears my burdens. Daily He provides strength to make the right choices. Daily I am free.**

_____

_____

_____

_____

_____

_____

_____

_____

_____

_____

_____

_____

_____

_____

_____

_____

_____

_____

_____

_____

*Philippians 4:13 NKJV   **Psalms 68:19

DAY 22

Iron Sharpens Iron

WISDOM FOR RELATIONSHIPS

WISDOM FOR TODAY

If one falls down, his friend can help him up.
But pity the man who falls And has no one to help him up!
Also, if two lie down together, they will keep warm. But how
can one keep warm alone? Though one may be overpowered,
Two can defend themselves A cord of three strands is not
quickly broken. Ecclesiastes. 4:10-12

What are the advantages of having friends?

_____

_____

_____

_____

_____

_____

_____

_____

_____

_____

_____

_____

_____

_____

_____

_____

Iron Sharpens Iron

God wants to break through to people with Godly wisdom. Why? Because it makes them successful. Wisdom brings success into our lives. And God wants us to have success in every area of our lives—including relationships. We were made to have relationships. We were not made to be hermits. Sometimes when everything is going wrong we think, *"I just want to run away, change my name, and get away from everybody."* But most likely, we wouldn't really like that. We might like it for one or two days, maybe even a week, but not for the long term. We were made for relationships.

Relationships are important for our growth. *Sophia* wisdom tells us that we are to be at peace with all men. That doesn't mean that we are going to like everybody and they are going to like us. However, the big picture is that we should have peace in our hearts and not envy, malice, hatred, and unforgiveness toward others. The big picture is God wants us to be like Him. He wants us to be merciful and gracious. The question is how? How can we do that?

The book of Proverbs is full of *Phronesis* wisdom (the how- to advice) about friendships and relationships. The words *friend* and *neighbor* are used interchangeably, but they basically have the same meaning. God handpicks certain people and brings them into our lives because He knows what they need, and He knows what we need. A friendship is a very creative thing.... it can create something bad or it can create something very wonderful.

Wisdom for Relationships

A friend can say or do something that really bothers us. We can get hurt and be angry or we can ask, "What does God want to create through this?" Does He want to do something in me? Does He want to bring up to the surface something I am doing that needs to be changed?"

When I first started in the ministry, I invited a certain woman to speak at a conference we were having and I became very upset because I felt as if she were using me. I expressed these feelings to the Lord and He asked me if I had ever used anyone. Well, I wasn't really talking about myself; I just wanted to talk about her. But God brought back to my remembrance some situations where I really had used people. God used that friendship to create in me humility and repentance.

It works both ways, good and bad. God would like to create through it, in whatever capacity we will allow Him. Look to Him to be the resource. We do not have the resources to create good things in everybody we meet...but God does. We need to look to God for His *Sophia* wisdom, for His understanding, for words of knowledge, for scripture and for ways we can create something good rather than something bad in our relationships.

> *Iron sharpens iron; so a man sharpens the countenance of his friend (to show rage or worthy purpose).* Proverbs 27:17, TAB

IRON SHARPENS IRON

One hard substance, such as a steel knife, whittled against another, such as stone, sharpens the edge. Just so, the collision of different minds sharpens each against the other. Sharp questions elicit sharp answers. Many valuable discoveries have come from the gathering of minds as they throw out ideas and suggestions. Sometimes a key thought comes to you from the chance statement of another, and from it the Lord gives you great ideas. We need others to sharpen our thinking. A good friend will stimulate productive thinking.

Sometimes a person becomes "dull" with the cares of this world or with adverse circumstances. He needs someone to sharpen him. In Malachi we read:

"Then those who feared the Lord spoke to one another,..." What do you suppose they said to one another? I'm sure they were encouraging one another in the Lord, because the scripture says:

> *"...the Lord gave attention and heard it, and a book of remembrance was written before Him for those who fear the Lord and who esteem His name."*
> Malachi 3:16

Do you realize that God is listening to every conversation you have with your friends? Are your conversations of the quality to which the Lord would give attention? When your friend is "dull", do your comments sharpen his thinking?

Wisdom for Relationships

God wants to use you to sharpen the soul of your friends, to stimulate them to good works, and to encourage them when the going gets rough.

...and let us consider how to stimulate one another to love and good deeds, not forsaking our own assembling together, as is the habit of some, but encouraging one another; and all the more, as you see the day drawing near. Hebrews 10:24, 25

Paul had friends who sharpened his countenance, and he was encouraged and able to minister effectively again.

And the brethren, when they heard about us, came from there as far as the Market of Appius and Three Inns to meet us; and when Paul saw them, he thanked God and took courage. Acts 28:15

Is there someone you know who always "rubs you the wrong way?" In light of the scripture, "Iron sharpens iron" what do you think God is trying to do through this relationship?

_____

_____

_____

_____

_____

Reflections

Today I am speaking these words over my life:

I provoke others unto love and good works.*

I speak the truth in love to my neighbors.**

_____
_____
_____
_____
_____
_____
_____
_____
_____
_____
_____
_____
_____
_____
_____
_____
_____
_____

*Hebrews 10:4   **Ephesians 4:15

Reflections

DAY 23

A Friend is...

WISDOM FOR RELATIONSHIPS

WISDOM FOR TODAY

"Where you go I will go, and where you stay I will stay. Your people will be my people and your God my God. Where you die I will die, and there I will be buried. May the LORD deal with me, be it ever so severely, if anything but death separates you and me." Ruth 1:16,17 NIV

     If ever Naomi needed a friend, it was during that trip! Her husband and both her sons were gone, and she would have been all alone in a strange country.

How did Ruth prove her friendship?

_____

_____

_____

_____

_____

Give an account of a specific moment in your life when someone proved their friendship to you.

_____

_____

_____

_____

_____

A Friend is...

The Bible says, *"Excellent speech is not becoming to a fool, much less lying lips to a prince."* A friend should speak good things to another friend. We should be able to exhort and encourage and not always be looking for someone to exhort and encourage us. Invariably, God will have us sow what we need in a friendship. He will have us sow into somebody else what we would like to have from another person.

When I was so sick some years ago with parasites, the Lord told me to call six sick people everyday and pray for them. These people were not even as sick as I was, but He said if I would sow, I would reap. So for days I looked for people who were sick to call. I still like to call people that are sick and pray for them. There is something in this that is so powerful, that we can sow into someone else and God will cause us to reap in unusual occasions.

> *Two are better than one, because they have a good (more satisfying) reward for their labor; for if they fall, the one will lift up his fellow. But woe to him who is alone when he falls and has not another to lift him up!* Ecclesiastes 4:9,10 TAB

We need friends. God designed us to need each other. He calls us the members of the Body of Christ. Each member depends on the others; they cannot function alone. God does not expect you to function without friends. That doesn't mean you look to people to supply your needs.

WISDOM FOR RELATIONSHIPS

No, God is your Source; but He uses people to deliver those supplies, and that includes fellowship and friendship. Ecclesiastes tells us that two are better than one because they have a more satisfying return on their labor. You can get a lot more done if you have a friend to help you!

Then, too, your friend is there to lift you up when you fall down. Have you ever stumbled and fallen, only to have a good friend come, pick you up, and help you on your way again? That's what friends are for!

> *A friend loves at all times, and a brother is born of adversity.* Proverbs 17:17

Friendship is based on several things such as common interests, close proximity, or similar experiences. Some friendships are intimate and lasting; others are shallow and fickle. What makes the difference? What makes a good friend? Or more specifically, how can you become a good, wise friend? Proverbs covers many subjects, and it has a great deal to say about the quality of friendship.

In Proverbs 17:17, we read that a friend loves at all times. This statement immediately rules out those "friends" who leave you when disaster strikes. Job's three friends would qualify on this point. They came as soon as they heard of Job's disaster, and they stayed with him—never left his side. They sat silently for seven days. That in itself was a test of true friendship. They came with good intentions: to sympathize and comfort him. When trouble came, they were there, ready to help their friend, Job.

> *Now when Job's three friends heard of all this adversity that had come upon him; they came each one from his own place, Eliphaz the Temanite, Bildad the Shuhite and Zophar the Naamathite; and they made an appointment together to come to sympathize with him and comfort him.....* Job 2:11

But did they love him? Love does not speak ill of his neighbor nor testify against him without cause. Love is not proud or puffed up; love is not boastful. Love thinks the best of a person, not the worst. These "friends "spent weeks showing Job why he was suffering, trying to get him to admit his guilt. Were they edifying him? No, Job was frustrated almost beyond endurance, and his friends gave him no relief. They stayed with him physically during the tragedy, but emotionally they were not with him. They were strengthening him, not really loving him.

> Job's assessment of his friends was, *"A despairing man should have the devotion of his friends even though he forsakes the fear of the Almighty. But my brothers are as undependable as intermittent streams,...Now you too have proved to be of no help; you see something dreadful and are afraid. You would even cast lots for the fatherless and barter away your friend."* Job 6:14,15,21,27, NIV

WISDOM FOR RELATIONSHIPS

Job needed friends who would love him at all times, especially during that time!

During his childhood, Joseph enjoyed the love and comradeship of his father, but he never really knew the friendship of his brothers. They were jealous of his relationship with his father. One day, in a fit of hatred, they sold him into slavery. For about 20 years, Joseph was either a slave or a prisoner. Could he ever be a friend to his brothers who had treated him so cruelly? Joseph was not one who had fed on resentment for years; his sustenance had been God's Word. He knew he was to be a ruler, and that's what kept him going.

When the day came for him to befriend his brothers, Joseph did it with style! Not only did he forgive his brothers and sell them the needed grain, but he also moved their entire households (70 of them) into Egypt! That family was literally saved from starvation by a brother who was born for that time of adversity and was faithful to fulfill his part as a friend.

What is God doing in relationships? He wants us to depend on Him as our source. Our friends may let us down but God doesn't. He doesn't want us to speak against them. He wants us to stand with them and build them up through encouraging words of truth and love.

A Friend is...

Think about a time when you let one of your friends down?
What could you have done differently?

_____

_____

_____

_____

_____

_____

_____

_____

_____

_____

_____

_____

_____

_____

_____

_____

_____

_____

_____

_____

_____

_____

_____

_____

_____

Reflections

Today I am speaking these words over my life:

I plant God's Word in the lives of others and I gain a great return.*

I lay down my life for my friends because Jesus lives in me.**

_____

_____

_____

_____

_____

_____

_____

_____

_____

_____

_____

_____

_____

_____

_____

_____

_____

_____

_____

_____

*Proverbs 12:14   **John 15:13

DAY 24

A Friend at Home

WISDOM FOR RELATIONSHIPS

WISDOM FOR TODAY

The wise woman builds her house, but with her own hands the foolish one tears hers down. Proverbs 14:1 NIV

What is your definition of a wise woman?

_____

_____

_____

_____

_____

_____

_____

_____

What areas in your home life do you need more wisdom for? How will you acquire this?

_____

_____

_____

_____

_____

_____

_____

_____

A FRIEND AT HOME

What kind of a friend should you be at home? What should you sow if you want to reap in a relationship? Back in the early years of my marriage, I was upset one time because I felt like my husband never told me I looked nice, or said anything good about the food I prepared. I remember complaining to the Lord about it, and the Lord said to me, "Well what do you say to him? Do you ever tell him he looks nice? Do you let him know how much you love cooking for him? Do you ever tell him he smells good? You never tell him anything good, so you don't reap anything good."

Some women are so bound up in meeting their own physical, emotional, and psychological needs that they have little time for their families. The liberated woman, however, knows who she is in Christ and is free to minister to her husband. *"She will comfort, encourage and do him only good as long as there is life within her."* Proverbs 31:12 TAB

She does him good! There are wives in the Bible who didn't! Eve "the helper" became the tempter:

> *Then the Lord God said, "It is not good for the man to be alone; I will make him a helper suitable for him."* Genesis 2:18

> *When the woman saw that the tree was good for food, and that it was a delight to the eyes, and that the tree was desirable to make one wise, she took from its fruit and ate; and she gave also to her husband with her, and he ate.* Genesis 3:6

WISDOM FOR RELATIONSHIPS

Job's wife advised her husband to curse God! *Then his wife said to him, "Do you still hold fast your integrity' Curse God and die!"* Job 2:9. She certainly was not encouraging and doing him good.

Jezebel incited her husband to do evil. *"Surely there was not one like Ahab who sold himself to do evil in the sight of the Lord, because Jezebel his wife incited him. "* I Kings 21:25

Rebekah helped her son deceive her husband (Genesis 27). Solomon's wives took him away from his God (1Kings11:15). These wives were not always blessings to their husbands!

Proverbs 31 gives us a picture of the excellent wife. She finds fulfillment in meeting her husband's needs. She is free to do that because she fears God and knows that her own needs are met. She is interested in her husband's needs, not just passively obeying. It would be easy for this wife's husband to follow Proverbs 5:15-23. He would enjoy drinking from his own cistern. Why? Because she does him good, comforts and encourages him. But it is also because she keeps herself attractive. His eyes aren't going to wander because at home his wife looks like a slob! He doesn't wander because this lady takes good care of her home and her body!

She makes coverings for herself; Her clothing is fine linen and purple. Proverbs 31:22

A FRIEND AT HOME

She encourages her husband to be everything he can be! What is the result? He is known at the city gates; he sits among the elders of the land. He is important!

"A virtuous and worthy wife—earnest and strong in character—is a crowning joy to her husband,..." Proverbs 12:4 TAB

He boasts of her, saying, "Many daughters have done nobly, but you excel them all." Proverbs 31:29

The biggest problem we have in all relationships is our mouth.

A constant dripping on a day of steady rain and a contentious woman are alike;... Proverbs 27:15

What a blessing it was for this man and his family not to be embarrassed by a quarrelsome woman! She was not like a constant dripping on a day of steady rain. Nor did he feel he had to live on the corner of the roof rather than live with a contentious wife. No, his wife spoke with wisdom and kindness. Her mouth proved she belonged to God and not to the world.

She opens her mouth with skillful and godly Wisdom, and in her tongue is the law of kindness—giving counsel and instruction. Proverbs 31:26 TAB

WISDOM FOR RELATIONSHIPS

She opens her mouth and speaks kindness. She also opens her hand to the poor and needy.

> *She extends her hand to the poor; and she stretches out her hands to the needy.* Proverbs 31:20

So it is very important that we see ourselves the way God wants us to be. God is using us, causing us to sow in order for us to reap. He who despises his neighbors sins, but he who has mercy on the poor is happy. Can you be merciful to the people that are unmerciful to you? Can you sow mercy?

_____

_____

_____

_____

_____

_____

_____

_____

_____

_____

_____

_____

_____

Reflections

Today I am speaking these words over my life:

I watch what I say and do not speak idle, careless words that bring discouragement or destruction.*

I speak words that bring life.**

_____
_____
_____
_____
_____
_____
_____
_____
_____
_____
_____
_____
_____
_____
_____
_____
_____
_____
_____

* Proverbs 12:18   **Matthew 12:34-37

Reflections

DAY 25

Choosing the Right Friends

WISDOM FOR RELATIONSHIPS

WISDOM FOR TODAY

A righteous man is cautious in friendship,
but the way of the wicked leads them astray.
Proverbs 12:26 NIV

What traits do you look for in a friend?

_____
_____
_____
_____
_____
_____
_____

How can you show yourself friendly to a new neighbor?

_____
_____
_____
_____
_____
_____
_____
_____
_____

Choosing the Right Friends

Choosing the right friends is so important, especially for children. If you have children or grandchildren, you need to pray the right friends in for them.

I was talking to my granddaughter one night before she went to bed and I asked about her friends. She sadly told me she didn't have any friends. I had never heard her say that before. She's a friendly person; I couldn't imagine why she didn't have any friends. So I suggested we pray. We prayed that she would know how to be a friend and that God would give her the right friends. Recently, I asked her again about her friends. This time she told me she had five friends, and I am praying that they are the right friends.

How can you choose the right friends? Listen to what God says; learn to hear the Holy Spirit. When I pray in the Spirit, it helps me listen better to the heart of a person and the words they are saying.

In the same way, the Spirit helps us in our weakness. We do not know what we ought to pray for, but the Spirit himself intercedes for us with groans that words cannot express. Romans 8:26 NIV

We don't know what to pray for but the Holy Spirit does. We don't know the big picture, but God does. He has *Sophia* wisdom; He sees the big picture.

WISDOM FOR RELATIONSHIPS

And we know that in all things God works for the good of those who love him, who have been called according to his purpose. Romans 8:28-29 NIV

When we pray in the Spirit, He searches our hearts and the hearts of others. When we pray according to God's will, He makes *all* things work together for good. Praying in the Spirit will give us wisdom for relationships.

What kind of friends have you chosen? Do you need God to give you wisdom on how to choose the right friends? Spend a few minutes in prayer right now and write down what God shows you about choosing friends.

_____

_____

_____

_____

_____

_____

_____

_____

_____

_____

_____

_____

_____

Reflections

Today I am speaking these words over my life:

I trust the Lord to guide me daily to make
decisions that line up with His character.*

I make wise choices because I choose the way of truth.**

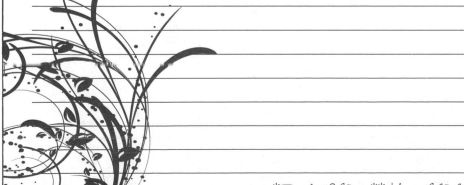

*Psalm 119:30   **Hebrews 13:20, 21

173

Reflections

DAY 26

Be Angry
and Sin Not

WISDOM FOR RELATIONSHIPS

WISDOM FOR TODAY

Do not let the sun go down while you are still angry,
And do not give the devil a foothold.
Ephesians 4:26-28 NIV

Describe a time that you went to bed angry. How did you feel? Did you sleep well?

_____
_____
_____
_____
_____
_____
_____
_____

What can you do to prevent going to bed angry?

_____
_____
_____
_____
_____
_____
_____

BE ANGRY AND SIN NOT!

The book of Proverbs is filled with *Phronesis* wisdom. It tells us how to choose our friends. Proverbs 22:24-25 advises us: *"Make no friendship with an angry man, and with a furious man do not go, lest you learn his ways and set a snare for your soul."*

If we hang around people that are always angry, always negative, always down on the establishment, pretty soon we will feel the same way. We won't be able to help them because we will be caught in the snare ourselves. When we hang around with angry people, they are creating something that is bad. We don't need the creation of that same anger in us. We don't need that friendship. We are not to argue hastily, but we are to settle for peace hastily.

> *Make friends quickly with your opponent at law while you are with him on the way, in order that your opponent may not deliver you to the judge, and the judge to the officer, and you be thrown into prison.* Mathew 5:25

We need to be so careful what we say about others when we find ourselves in a conflict. Even if our neighbor is wrong, we should not speak about it to others. The people who are involved in the situation might know of the matter; but no others need to. This is an area where the spiritual fruit of self-control becomes important.

Wisdom for Relationships

Let no unwholesome word proceed from your mouth, but only such a word as is good for edification according to the need of the moment, that it may give grace to those who hear. Ephesians 4:29

Do not complain, brethren, against one another, that you yourselves may not be judged; behold, the Judge is standing right at the door. James 5:9

Also, we cannot just ignore people who have caused us pain. There must be a positive action on our part if we are to fully obey God. If we continue to think of a person in terms of the wrong he did to us, we are feeding a spark of revenge that could flare up years from now. Remember Absalom? His sister, Tamar, was raped by his half brother. Instead of confronting Amnon and settling the issue, he was quiet about it and acted like he was ignoring the incident. But for two full years, he planned revenge. One day he invited all his brothers to a sheep-shearing party, and while Amnon was drunk, Absalom had his servants kill him. His revenge was murder.

Then Absalom her brother said to her, "Has Amnon your brother been with you? But now keep silent, my, sister, he is your brother; do not take this matter to heart." So Tamar remained and was desolate in her brother Absalom's house. II Samuel 13:20

BE ANGRY AND SIN NOT!

And Absolam commanded his servants, saying, "See now, when Amnon's heart is merry with wine, and when I say to you, 'Strike Amnon,' then put him to to death. Do not hear; have not I myself commanded you? Be courageous and be valiant." II Samuel 13:28

Absolam should have waited for God to rightfully execute judgment upon Amnon.

We don't have to trust our enemies, but we are bound to love them, do good to them, and forgive them. That's God's Word! Elisha set a good example of feeding his enemies. The king of Aram was enraged by the prophet because he kept helping the Israeli king by warning him of every ambush. As soon as the king of Aram discovered who was responsible for his failures, he sent a large army with horses and chariots to surround the city of Dothan, where Elisha was.

Elisha's servant was frightened because the enemy looked great and fearsome, but when Elisha prayed that the servant's eyes would be opened, he saw the hills surrounding Elisha full of chariots of fire. God's army was bigger than the enemy's. Then Elisha prayed that the enemy's army would be blinded. God answered, and they were surrounded by a helpless, blind army. Elisha led them to the king of Israel, and when their eyes were opened, they were inside Samaria. (What an opportunity for revenge!)

WISDOM FOR RELATIONSHIPS

The king of Israel said, "Shall I kill them?"
Obviously, the answer would be yes—an easy,
supernatural victory! But Elisha said, "No, give them
food and water and send them back to their master."
What a way to treat your personal enemies! The result?
The bands from Aram stopped raiding Israel's territory
(II Kings 6:8-22). God's way worked! Elisha and all
of Israel never had any more trouble with that enemy
again! Revenge doesn't conquer an enemy's heart, but
love does!

Sometimes, even in our homes, members of
our family may temporarily act like an enemy. God's
instructions are clear:

> *Not returning evil for evil, or insult for insult, but*
> *giving a blessing instead; for you were called for*
> *the very purpose that you might inherit a blessing.*
> I Peter 3:9

God promises to reward you when you bless those who
curse you and love those who hate you!

BE ANGRY AND SIN NOT!

Think about a time when a friend complained to you about someone who wronged him. How did you feel about the person who wronged your friend? What did you say about the situation? Should you have acted differently?

_____

_____

_____

_____

_____

_____

_____

_____

_____

_____

_____

_____

_____

_____

_____

_____

_____

_____

_____

_____

_____

_____

_____

_____

_____

_____

Reflections

Today I am speaking these words over my life:

I am slow to speak and slow to anger. I listen carefully and think before I speak.*

I put away all bitterness and anger and am kind to others.**

_____

_____

_____

_____

_____

_____

_____

_____

_____

_____

_____

_____

_____

_____

_____

_____

_____

_____

_____

_____

_____

_____

*James 1:19   **Ephesians 4:31-32

DAY 27

Is that a "Speck" in Your Eye?

WISDOM FOR RELATIONSHIPS

WISDOM FOR TODAY

*And why do you look at the speck in your brother's eye,
but do not consider the plank in your own eye? Or how
can you say to your brother, 'Let me remove the speck from
your eye'; and look, a plank is in your own eye? Hypocrite!
First remove the plank from your own eye, and then you will
see clearly to remove the speck from your brother's eye.*
Matthew 7:3-5

The Pharisees and teachers of the law brought a woman
to Jesus who was caught in the act of adultery. However,
Jesus was more concerned with the "plank" in their own
eyes as He wrote upon the ground.

What "plank" was in their eyes?

_____

_____

_____

_____

_____

_____

_____

_____

_____

_____

Is that a Speck in Your Eye?

What happens when we associate with people who have been "offended"? If we are not careful, we will pick up their offense and carry it with them. Our feelings about the person that offended them change. When we listen to someone who is offended, we only hear their side of the story. We don't know the whole situation, and most importantly, we don't know what God wants to do through it. We just pick up their offense and it begins to set a snare in our own mind and emotions.

There are times when we all need someone we can let our hair down with, however, we need to make sure it is someone who will tell us the truth and will pray with us so it doesn't create a snare in them.

> *Do not be a witness against your neighbor without cause, And do not deceive with your lips.*
> Proverbs 24:28

Doeg had opportunity to witness against his "neighbor" David. David had done him no wrong, yet Doeg *"loved evil more than good."* (Read Psalm 52 concerning David's feelings about Doeg.) When Saul wanted to know the whereabouts of David, Doeg witnessed against him, telling of his visit to Ahimelech, the priest, and how he was fed and given a sword. The result was Saul's order to massacre all the priests of Nob. The only one who would carry out the order was Doeg He began with a witness against his neighbor and ended up murdering God's priests.

Wisdom for Relationships

Then Doeg the Edomite, who was standing by the servants of Saul, answered and said, "I saw the son of Jesse coming to Nob, to Ahimelech the son of Ahitub. And he inquired of the Lord for him, gave him provisions, and gave him the sword of Goliath the Philistine." I Samuel 22:9,10

Then the king said to Doeg, "You turn around and attack the priests." And Doeg the Edomite turned around and attacked the priests and killed that day eighty-five men who wore the linen ephod.
I Samuel 22:18

Obviously, every witness against a neighbor doesn't end in murder, but a witness without a cause comes out of hate. And God says, *"Everyone who hates his brother is a murderer."* I John 3:15a.

Our lips should never cause harm to our neighbors; they should be speaking things to edify and build up. If there is need to witness against our neighbors, it must be the truth and for their correction and help, never out of revenge or malice.

Is that a Speck in Your Eye?

Think about a time you were snared by an offense? How did it happen? Have you removed the "plank" from your eye? If not, what steps can you take now to remove it?

_____

_____

_____

_____

_____

_____

_____

_____

_____

_____

_____

_____

_____

_____

_____

_____

_____

_____

_____

_____

_____

_____

_____

_____

_____

_____

_____

_____

Reflections

Today I am speaking these words over my life:

I reject every manifestation of pride, strife, and rebellion in my life. I esteem others as better than myself. I do nothing out of strife or vain glory.*

I do not judge others or put a stumbling block in their way.**

_____
_____
_____
_____
_____
_____
_____
_____
_____
_____
_____
_____
_____
_____
_____
_____
_____
_____
_____

*Philippians 2:3   **Romans 14:13

DAY 28

Blind Spot Ahead

WISDOM FOR RELATIONSHIPS

WISDOM FOR TODAY

*Let each one of us make it a practice to please (make happy)
his neighbor for his good and for his true welfare,
to edify him—that is, to strengthen him and build
him up spiritually.* Romans 15:2 TAB

We want to please others, especially our friends. God
commends this. He does not wish us to be selfishly looking
only to our own affairs; He expects us to look for ways to
please our neighbors. How can we do that?

_____

_____

_____

_____

_____

_____

_____

_____

_____

_____

_____

_____

_____

_____

_____

_____

_____

_____

Blind Spot Ahead

I love that the Bible deals with every kind of relationship we could ever have. We don't have to try to figure it out by ourselves. Proverbs reveals the *Phronesis* how-to wisdom, and we know God in His big *Sophia* wisdom knows how to network (*Sunesis* wisdom) the right people in and the wrong people out. God knows how to do it. He advises us to be direct with people, not cruel, and to speak the truth in love. We should be able to confront others and speak candidly.

Proverbs 27:6 says, *"Faithful are the wounds of a friend, but the kisses of an enemy are deceitful."* A good friend wants to create truth and honesty in you. We might get mad for a moment, however, we need to realize their purpose was to help us.

At one point, Paul felt like the Galatians had ceased to be his friends. Early in their relationship, they would have given their eyes to help him. Later, however, when he was correcting them concerning their regression into bondage to the law, he asked them if he had become their enemy by telling them the truth. They had difficulty receiving correction from him.

> *I beg of you, brethren, become as I am, for I also have become as you are. You have done me not wrong; but you know that it was because of a bodily illness that I preached the gospel to you the first time; and that which was a trial to you in my bodily condition*

you did not despise or loathe, but you received me as an angel of God, as Christ Jesus Himself. Where then is that sense of blessing you had? For I bear witness, that if possible, you would have plucked out your eyes and given them to me. Have I therefore become your enemy by telling you the truth? Galatians 4:12-16

Those who did receive rebuke grew in the Lord and grew in their love for Paul. Honesty is imperative in a wise, healthy friendship.

Paul and Peter were friends. They served the same God and were called to the same ministry. One was called to the Gentiles, the other to the Jews. They preached the same Gospel, and they practiced the same principles— almost the same. At one point, Paul saw that Peter was preaching right but wasn't practicing right. Did Paul turn his head and look the other way? No, he loved Peter too much to do that. With confidence that came from true love, he openly rebuked Peter for refusing to eat with the Gentiles when the Jewish leaders were present.

If we are to be a true friend, occasionally we will be called upon to point out a blind spot. Sometimes the quickest way to grow is to remove the hindrances!

BLIND SPOT AHEAD

Have you noticed a "blind spot" in one of your friends?
How can you help them to see it?

_____

_____

_____

_____

_____

_____

_____

_____

_____

_____

_____

_____

_____

_____

_____

_____

_____

_____

_____

_____

_____

_____

_____

_____

_____

_____

Reflections

Today I am speaking these words over my life:

God is completing the work that He began in me.*

I bear others' burdens and fulfill the law of Christ.**

_____

_____

_____

_____

_____

_____

_____

_____

_____

_____

_____

_____

_____

_____

_____

_____

_____

_____

_____

*Philippians 1:6   **Galatians 6:2

DAY 29

Open Rebuke vs. Secret Love

WISDOM FOR RELATIONSHIPS

WISDOM FOR TODAY

*He who rebukes a man will afterward find more
favor than he who flatters with the tongue.*
Proverbs 28:23

Friends are more than companions who share our interests
and goals, laugh at our jokes, think we're great, and enjoy
spending time with us. Friends see our blind spots; and if
they are true friends they point them out to us. What "blind
spot" has a friend pointed out to you recently?

_____

_____

_____

_____

_____

_____

You show you are a wise friend by receiving rebuke. It takes
God's love to receive rebuke as well as to give it. How do
you react when a friend tries to correct you?

_____

_____

_____

_____

_____

Open Rebuke vs. Secret Love

Proverbs 27:5 states, *"open rebuke is better than love carefully concealed."* I don't think that when somebody is rebuking me, do you? Do you think people are just thrilled to receive rebuke? I don't think so. And yet this is the biblical way we should behave.

We had a friend who was a well-known evangelist, and when his wife left him some pastors quit inviting him to speak at their churches. He hadn't done anything wrong, wasn't living immorally, but people just dropped him. God dealt with my husband and me to be his friend. During that time, I received an invitation to speak in a big church, and the pastor called me to ask if I was a friend of the evangelist. When I responded yes to that question, he revoked his invitation and avoided me for years. Sometimes, we are called to be a friend even when it is not convenient. God wants us to create some love in those people who are so despondent.

> *Your oils have a pleasing fragrance, Your name is like purified oil; Therefore the maidens love you.*
> Song of Solomon 1:3

A friend's faithfulness is felt when he points out your blind spots, and the sweetness of his friendship is tasted in his wise counsel. David and Jonathan had that kind of frendship. Jonathan risked his life to tell David that it was not safe to return to the palace. Their conversation was

WISDOM FOR RELATIONSHIPS

always mutually uplifting. Even though Jonathan's father hated David, he was faithful to his friend. Once when it was very obvious that Saul was seeking to kill David, Jonathan made a special trip to encourage him. Jonathan spoke positive words to David that reflected the promises of God. He encouraged him with the Word. No counsel is sweeter than the Word of God.

Sweet counsel is counsel that helps, that meets the need of the moment. Moses received the counsel of his father-in-law; it was sweet to him because it met his need, relieving him of the pressure of leading two million people. (Exodus 18:17-24)

Is God calling you to rebuke someone you love? How can you always give counsel that is sweet?

_____

_____

_____

_____

_____

_____

_____

_____

_____

_____

Reflections

Today I am speaking these words over my life:

I am open to Godly reproof and wisdom.*

I am bringing forth the peaceable fruit of righteousness.**

_____

_____

_____

_____

_____

_____

_____

_____

_____

_____

_____

_____

_____

_____

_____

_____

_____

_____

_____

_____

*Isaiah 32:17.   **Proverbs 15:5

Reflections

DAY 30

Reconciliation

WISDOM FOR RELATIONSHIPS

WISDOM FOR TODAY

All this is from God, who reconciled us to himself through Christ and gave us the ministry of reconciliation: that God was reconciling the world to himself in Christ, not counting men's sins against them. 2 Cor 5:18-19 NIV

What does having 'the ministry of reconciliation" mean to you?

_____

_____

_____

_____

_____

_____

_____

God wants to use you to bring reconciliation to others. Can you think of someone God wants you to minister to?

_____

_____

_____

_____

_____

_____

_____

_____

RECONCILIATION

Aren't you glad that you can be a creator of good things and not bad; that you can create good things in others even if they are being ugly to you? Always try to bring unity. *How good and pleasant it is when brothers live together in unity !* Psalms 133:1 NIV.

I have prayed Colossians 1:20 over and over for broken relationships, even broken marriages, and have seen them healed. Colossians 1:20 states: *"And by Him to reconcile all things to Himself, by Him, whether things on earth or things in heaven having made peace through the blood of the cross."* Reconciliation comes through the blood of Jesus. The blood of Jesus can bring peace. I can repent of anything I have done wrong to another person and the blood of Jesus will bring peace between us. Therefore, I can ask that the blood of Jesus would bring peace for a husband and wife.

We had a woman in our church who left her husband, ran off with another man, and took their five children with her. The husband took Colossians 1:20 and believed that God would reconcile them. He repented of anything he had done wrong and when he came to church, he would just speak wonderful things about her, even though she would curse him on the phone. About a year and half later, she called him and said she wanted to come home if he would still have her. The blood of Jesus brought peace in him.

WISDOM FOR RELATIONSHIPS

Today, if you're bitter because of something a person did to you, you need to repent and ask that the blood of Jesus cleanse you from unforgiveness and bring peace to you. Write down your prayer of reconciliation.

_____

_____

_____

_____

_____

_____

_____

_____

_____

_____

_____

_____

_____

_____

_____

_____

_____

_____

_____

Reflections

Today I am speaking these words over my life:

Every day I spread God's knowledge
to someone.*

I have been given the ministry of reconciliation.**

_____
_____
_____
_____
_____
_____
_____
_____
_____
_____
_____
_____
_____
_____
_____
_____
_____

*Proverbs 15:7   **2 Corinthians 5:19

Reflections

DAY 31

What Kind of Friend am I?

WISDOM FOR RELATIONSHIPS

WISDOM FOR TODAY

"Blessed is the man who listens to me, Watching daily at My gates, Waiting at my doorposts." Proverbs 8:34

When was the last time you spent time waiting at His gates? What happened?

_____

_____

_____

_____

_____

_____

_____

God will speak to you if you take time to listen. Take a few minutes now to wait upon Him and write what He is telling you.

_____

_____

_____

_____

_____

_____

_____

_____

WHAT KIND OF FRIEND AM I?

The book of Proverbs is filled with *Phronesis* wisdom or practical advice about friendships and relationships. You might laugh because some of these sayings are just common sense, but maybe you will see some things that you need to practice.

Proverbs 25:17 admonishes us: *"Seldom set foot in your neighbor's house lest he come weary of you and hate you."* If you are always going over to someone's house, you'd better make sure they want you there. People get tired of someone coming to their house all the time. Everybody needs privacy; everyone needs personal time.

A few years after we started our first church, there was a couple who would always drop in on us on Saturday night. I had to bathe the children and get their clothes ready for Sunday morning. I taught Sunday school at that time, so I had to prepare my lesson as well as get my own clothing ready. It was a busy time. Every Saturday night, in the midst of this, they would show up just to visit; it was not a positive thing. Finally, Wally and I had to sit them down and explain that Saturday night was not a good night for us. We had to tell them in order to save our friendship, and they are still our friends today. Avoid over-staying your welcome.

WISDOM FOR RELATIONSHIPS

I had a very good friend who shared with me that when her daughter got married, she asked her future son-in-law what they could do to be a blessing. He asked them not to make frequent visits during the first year of their marriage. She was not hurt by his request at all. It was good advice. Once we become in-laws, we should call our children if we want to visit to see if it is a convenient time for them. We need to go at their invitation.

Because we love our neighbors, we need to be considerate of their time and privacy, allowing them the courtesy of calls that have purpose, not just the passing of time. We should make our visits valuable and a blessing by not making them too often or too long.

The book of Proverbs is full of these practical one-line gems! Read one chapter of Proverbs and write down all the practical advice you find there.

_____

_____

_____

_____

_____

_____

_____

_____

_____

_____

Reflections

Today I am speaking these words over my life:

I listen to Godly counsel and am open to the voice
of the Holy Spirit.*

I love my neighbors as myself and therefore, do no harm
to them.**

_____

_____

_____

_____

_____

_____

_____

_____

_____

_____

_____

_____

_____

_____

_____

_____

_____

_____

_____

*Psalms 32:8, John 10:27   **Romans 13:9-10

Reflections

DAY 32

Sensitive Situations

WISDOM FOR RELATIONSHIPS

WISDOM FOR TODAY

So in everything, do to others what you would have them do to you, for this sums up the Law and the Prophets.
Matthew 7:12 NIV

Think about a time when someone was insensitive to your needs. How did it make you feel? How did you react towards them?

_____

_____

_____

_____

_____

_____

_____

List several ways you can be more considerate of others.

_____

_____

_____

_____

_____

_____

_____

SENSITIVE SITUATIONS

Examples of sensitive situations are sprinkled throughout the book of Proverbs. *"He who blesses his friend with a loud voice early in the morning, it will be reckoned a curse to him."* Proverbs 27:14

Be sensitive to other people's schedule. Just because you are an early riser doesn't mean the whole world is awake. You may be up singing *"This is the day the Lord has made, I will be glad and rejoice in it"* but if you decide to call a friend too early, they certainly are not going to be glad and rejoice that you are their friend.

Whenever I am not traveling and I am at home, I try to stay on a regular schedule. I go to bed early, because I get up so early. I went to bed early the other night and was asleep by 9:30. Unfortunately, someone called me at 9:30 and woke me from a sound sleep. She just wanted to visit, nothing important. I was honest with her and told her I was sleeping. She had not thought that anyone would be asleep at that time. I explained that I go to bed early but I also get up at 4:30 in the morning.

Not everyone enjoys waking up to a happy shout! Be a good friend. Find out what "pleases" them in the morning. Many a loud voice is not welcome, so keep it quiet. Remember, love is kind!

Be sensitive to schedules and also to where people are emotionally or spiritually. *"Rejoice with those who rejoice, and weep with those who weep. "* Romans 12:15

WISDOM FOR RELATIONSHIPS

Like one who takes off a garment on a cold day, or like vinegar on soda, is he who sings songs to a troubled heart. Proverbs 25:20

Cheerful songs are not always welcome. There is a time to rejoice with those who rejoice, but there is also a time to weep with those who weep. If you are joyfully singing to the troubled heart, it is like taking away his coat in cold weather. (This is an act of cruelty that was forbidden by God. You should not take the poor man's coat.)

Do you have a friend who is going through a hard time and is struggling with finances, health issues, or problems with their children? What can you do to help that person?

_____

_____

_____

_____

_____

_____

_____

_____

_____

_____

_____

Reflections

Today I am speaking these words over my life:

I am wise. I hear the Lord's voice. I am increasing
in learning and becoming a man/woman of understanding.*

I am kind and compassionate to others and forgive just as
Christ forgave me.**

_____

_____

_____

_____

_____

_____

_____

_____

_____

_____

_____

_____

_____

_____

_____

_____

**Proverbs 1:5   **Ephesians 4:33

Reflections

DAY 33

To Co-sign or Not to Co-sign

WISDOM FOR RELATIONSHIPS

WISDOM FOR TODAY

He who puts up security for another will surely suffer, but whoever refuses to strike hands in pledge is safe.
Proverbs 11:15 NIV

Did you ever ask anyone to co-sign for you, or give you a loan? Were you faithful to pay back your debt? How long did it take?

_____

_____

_____

_____

_____

_____

_____

_____

_____

_____

_____

_____

_____

_____

_____

_____

_____

_____

To Co-sign or Not to Co-sign

The answer to that question is plain and simple: Don't cosign for people! What if someone comes to you and asks to borrow ten thousand dollars? They don't have the assets to back it up but they are asking you because they know you have the money.

Did you know the Bible gives explicit instruction about this?   Four times in the book of Proverbs it says don't co-sign, four times!

> *My son, if you have put up security for your neighbor,*
> *if you have struck hands in pledge for another,*
> *if you have been trapped by what you said,*
> *ensnared by the words of your mouth,*
> Proverbs 6:1-2 NIV

> *He who puts up security for another will surely suffer,*
> *but whoever refuses to strike hands in pledge is safe.*
> Proverbs 11:15 NIV

> *A man lacking in judgment strikes hands in pledge*
> *and puts up security for his neighbor.*
> Proverbs 17:18 NIV

> *Do not be a man who strikes hands in pledge*
> *or puts up security for debts;*
> *if you lack the means to pay,*
> *your very bed will be snatched from under you.*
> Proverbs 22:26-27 NIV

WISDOM FOR RELATIONSHIPS

Proverbs 6:3-5 offers some *Phronesis* wisdom in case you have already done it. But specifically the admonition is to get out of it.

then do this, my son, to free yourself,
since you have fallen into your neighbor's hands:
Go and humble yourself;
press your plea with your neighbor!
Allow no sleep to your eyes,
no slumber to your eyelids.
Free yourself, like a gazelle from the hand of the hunter,
like a bird from the snare of the fowler.
Proverbs 6:3-5 NIV

Do everything you can to get out of it, be warm, be friendly, but don't rest until you get out of it.

A dear friend shared her story with me. She started dating a man whom she liked very much. He seemed so wonderful, and he loved her children. He asked her for a loan or to co-sign a loan for him for a short period of time. Not too much money, just $2,300. She said that she knew inside that she shouldn't, but she did it anyway. After she co-signed the loan, he dumped her. That was three years ago, and he hasn't paid it back yet. She learned a hard lesson.

To Co-sign or Not to Co-sign

It's easy to fall into the snare of co-signing if you are a compassionate person and want to meet people's needs. We try to be the ultimate solution to everybody and everything. However, when you co-sign for people who don't pay their bills you are not helping them; you are enabling them. You are taking out of your own pocket and in the end, you will suffer for it.

God did not call you to be a co-signer for other people. Jesus is the co-signer, He became a surety for us, He co-signed for our sins, and He co-signed for our sicknesses. He co-signed because He has plenty to back it up. He said I will take your sins and I will cleanse you with my blood. I will take your sicknesses and I will give you my health. There is a co-signer who is wonderful and creates good things in us—Jesus Christ. He can meet your need in a special way so you won't get caught up in that snare.

Although you often want to help your loved ones or friends by co-signing for them, why should you refuse? Write several scenarios that can happen and the effect they would have on you.

_____

_____

_____

_____

_____

_____

Reflections

Today I am speaking these words over my life:

I will know the truth and the truth will set me free.*

I refuse to put up security for others' debts.**

_____

_____

_____

_____

_____

_____

_____

_____

_____

_____

_____

_____

_____

_____

_____

_____

_____

_____

_____

_____

*John 8:32   **Proverbs 22:26

DAY 34

Only Joking!

WISDOM FOR RELATIONSHIPS

WISDOM FOR TODAY

*People who shrug off deliberate deceptions, saying,
"I didn't mean it, I was only joking," Are worse than
Careless campers who walk away from smoldering
campfires.* Proverbs 26:18-19 MSG

Have you ever been the brunt of a practical joke? What
happened? How did it make you feel? Did it have any
lasting effects?

_____

_____

_____

_____

_____

_____

_____

_____

_____

_____

_____

_____

_____

_____

_____

ONLY JOKING!

"Like a madman who throws firebrands, arrows and death, so is the man who deceives his neighbor, and says, "Was I not joking?" Proverbs 26:18-19

Some jokes just aren't funny because they go too far. Proverbs says they are like the work of a madman. A madman might not be accountable for his actions, but we are! Good friends don't carry a joke to the point of hurting someone. Paul advised that *"...there must be no filthiness and silly talk, or coarse jesting, which are not fitting...."* Ephesians 5:4.

During my first year of college I lived at home and went to school at night, but for my sophomore year I moved on campus. We couldn't get in the dorms because they were too full, so we had a college-approved house. There were twelve of us, and I was the youngest. I loved playing practical jokes on people. I would paint bars of soap with clear nail polish so when my house mates would try to rub their hands on their soap, it didn't come off. I put Saran Wrap over the commode during the night I could short sheet beds faster than anybody in the world. Finally after about three months, the girls were really getting tired of this and they told me it was time to stop. They were very candid with me and I needed it. Don't carry a joke too far!

WISDOM FOR RELATIONSHIPS

Have you noticed how explicit Proverbs gets with every subject it covers? Friendship is a very precious thing. Value your friends; treat them the way Jesus would. Extend your hand of friendship to those who need it most. Jesus said if you invite only those who will invite you back, what value is that? Extend your invitations to those who cannot return them. Offer your friendship to someone who has nothing to give in return. That's what Jesus did!

Write about a time when a friend honestly told you something you needed to change? Did you take heed to that advice? What might have happened if you weren't teachable?

_____

_____

_____

_____

_____

_____

_____

_____

_____

_____

_____

_____

Reflections

Today I am speaking these words over my life:

I apply my heart to discipline and my ears
to knowledge.*

I do not partake in foolish talk or coarse joking,**

_____
_____
_____
_____
_____
_____
_____
_____
_____
_____
_____
_____
_____
_____
_____
_____
_____
_____
_____

*Proverbs 23:12   **Ephesians 5:4

Reflections

DAY 35

Closer than a Brother

WISDOM FOR RELATIONSHIPS

WISDOM FOR TODAY

A man of many friends may come to ruin, but there is
friend who sticks closer than a brother.
Proverbs 18:24 NIV

Describe your relationship with your best friend.

_____

_____

_____

_____

_____

_____

Have you ever been betrayed by a friend? What happened?
How did you feel?

_____

_____

_____

_____

_____

_____

_____

CLOSER THAN A BROTHER

If you want to have a friend, show yourself friendly. If you don't have friends, there is a friend who sticks closer than a brother. His name is Jesus! Jesus called Judas a friend even though He knew Judas was about to betray Him. I wouldn't have called him a friend; I would have called him a thug. Even in Psalms there is a prophecy about Judas which says *"my own familiar friend in whom I trusted who ate my bread."* Why do you think Jesus called Judas a friend? He was trying to create a new life in Judas. It didn't happen, but Jesus always stayed in that place of relationship.

Luke was a friend of Paul and he was also a physician. He practiced his medicine while he was on missionary journeys with Paul, and they prayed for the sick. When Paul was imprisoned, they allowed him to have two slaves with him. History tells us that Luke became a slave so he could serve Paul in prison. He practiced his medicine while he was with Paul, and they prayed for the sick. What a relationship they must have had.

Jesus was not ashamed to call us brethren. He shared our flesh and blood, and He shared our temptations.

For both He who sanctifies and those who are sanctified are all from one father; for which reason He is not ashamed to call them brethren. Hebrews 2:11

Wisdom for Relationships

For God so loved the world that He gave His only begotten Son, that whoever believes in Him should not perish, but have eternal life. John 3:16

He came to earth because of love, and He loved us so much, He laid down His life for us.

Now before the Feast of the Passover, Jesus knowing that His hour had come that He would depart out of this world to the Father, having loved His own who were in the world, He loved them to the end. John 13:1 NIV

Greater love has no one than this that one lay down his life for his friends. You are My friends, if you do what I command you. NO longer do I call you slaves; for the slave does not know what his master is doing; but I have called you friends, for all things that I have heard from my Father I have made known to you." John 15:13-15 NASB

…teaching them to observe all that I commanded you; and lo, I am with you always, even to the end of the age. Mathew 28:20 NASB

Jesus is your constant and eternal Friend. He is with you in times of adversity, and His love is never diluted. He loves you whether you deserve it or not; He is always loyal to you. No matter how unfaithful you are, He is always faithful to His Word for you. In a very real sense, Jesus is the Brother "born for adversity," for no circumstance is too great for him. No matter how many other friends desert you, He never will. Truly, Jesus is your Friend who sticks closer than a brother.

We are Christ in this world, filled with confidence and the love of God. His love in us reaches out to the friend in need. His love in us reaches out with deed and truth, not just words.

By this, love is perfected with us, that we may have confidence in the Day of Judgment; because as He is, so also are we in this world. I John 4:17

But whoever has the world's goods, and beholds his brother in need and closes his heart against him, how does the love of God abide in him? Little children, let us not love with word or with tongue, but in deed and truth.   I John 3:17-18

WISDOM FOR RELATIONSHIPS

It takes work to maintain any relationship. If our
relationship with Jesus is lacking, it will affect all our
relationships. What specific things can you do to
improve your relationship with Jesus?

_____

_____

_____

_____

_____

_____

_____

_____

_____

_____

_____

_____

_____

_____

_____

_____

_____

_____

_____

_____

_____

_____

_____

_____

_____

Reflections

Today I am speaking these words over my life:

I walk with integrity, work righteousness, and speak the truth in my heart.*

I love others because I am born of God and God is love.**

*Psalms 15:2 **I John 4:7-8

Reflections